IMMIGRATION IN THE 21ST CENTURY: POLITICAL, SOCIAL AND ECONOMIC ISSUES

IMMIGRATION POLICY PROPOSALS AND POTENTIAL BUDGETARY EFFECTS

IMMIGRATION IN THE 21ST CENTURY: POLITICAL, SOCIAL AND ECONOMIC ISSUES

Additional books in this series can be found on Nova's website under the Series tab.

Additional e-books in this series can be found on Nova's website under the e-book tab.

CONTENTS

PREFACE

This book examines some of those proposals and how such changes would affect the federal budget.

Chapter 1 – During the past two years, the Congress has considered proposals to modify the nation's immigration system. The Border Security, Economic Opportunity, and Immigration Modernization Act (S. 744), passed by the Senate in June 2013, addresses multiple facets of immigration policy, including changes to the existing visa system, improvements in border security and law enforcement, and changes to the status of people who currently live in the country without legal authorization. Other proposals have focused on one component of immigration policy— for example, improving border security or changing certain aspects of the visa system. Whether the proposals involve broad or narrow changes to immigration policy, they could have a variety of consequences for both citizens and noncitizens, for the federal government, and for state and local governments. This Congressional Budget Office (CBO) report examines some of those proposals and how such changes would affect the federal budget.

When estimating the budgetary consequences of immigration reform, CBO considers various factors. Depending on the details of proposed legislation, changes to immigration policy could have a significant effect on the size and composition of the noncitizen population and, as a result, on rates of participation in federal programs and the payment of taxes. For that reason, when estimating the budgetary effects of proposals, CBO considers the demographic and labor force characteristics of foreign-born people, their eligibility for and participation in federal programs, their tax liability, changes in the economy, and a number of other factors. If proposals were combined into a single, more comprehensive immigration bill, estimates of the budgetary effects would take into account the complex interactions among the various provisions; the net effect would not be a simple summation of the individual effects.

Chapter 2 – Immigration reform was an active legislative issue in the first session of the 113th Congress. The Senate passed the Border Security, Economic Opportunity, and Immigration Modernization Act (S. 744), a comprehensive immigration reform bill that includes provisions on border security, interior enforcement, employment eligibility verification and worksite enforcement, legalization of unauthorized aliens, immigrant visas, nonimmigrant visas, and humanitarian admissions. For its part, the House took a different approach to immigration reform. Rather than considering a single comprehensive bill, the House acted on a set of immigration bills that address border security, interior enforcement, employment eligibility verification and worksite enforcement, and nonimmigrant and immigrant visas. House committees reported or ordered to be reported the following immigration bills: Border Security Results Act of 2013 (H.R. 1417); Strengthen and Fortify Enforcement (SAFE) Act (H.R. 2278); Legal Workforce Act (H.R. 1772); Agricultural Guestworker (AG) Act (H.R. 1773); and Supplying Knowledge-based Immigrants and Lifting Levels of STEM Visas (SKILLS Visa) Act (H.R. 2131).

Beyond their work on immigration reform legislation, the House and Senate acted on other immigration-related bills. Among these measures, the 113th Congress passed the Violence Against Women Reauthorization Act of 2013 (P.L. 113-4), which includes provisions on noncitizen victims of domestic abuse or certain other crimes and on victims of human trafficking. Other immigration issues addressed in enacted measures include Iraqi and Afghan special immigrants (P.L. 113-42, P.L. 113-66, P.L. 113-76, P.L. 113-160), refugees (P.L. 113-6, P.L. 113-76), temporary nonagricultural workers (P.L. 113-76, P.L. 113-164), international adoption (P.L. 113- 74), and alien inadmissibility (P.L. 113-100).

Several bills passed one house of Congress, but not the other. In addition to the comprehensive immigration reform bill (S. 744), the Senate passed measures dealing with border security personnel compensation (S. 1691), the application of immigration law in the Commonwealth of the Northern Mariana Islands (CNMI) (S. 1237), and the visa waiver program (S. 2673). House-passed measures address, among other issues, border security and unaccompanied alien children (UAC) arriving in the United States (H.R. 5230), human trafficking (H.R. 3530, H.R. 3610, H.R. 5135), prosecutorial discretion (H.R. 2217, H.R. 5272), and the visa waiver program (H.R. 938).

This report discusses these and other immigration-related issues that received legislative action or have been of significant congressional interest in the 113th Congress.

Chapter 3 – On November 20, 2014, President Obama announced his Immigration Accountability Executive Action which revises some U.S. immigration policies and initiates several programs, including a revised border security policy for the Southwest border; deferred action programs for some unauthorized aliens; revised interior enforcement priorities; changes to aid the entry of skilled workers; the promotion of immigrant integration and naturalization; and several other initiatives the President indicated would improve the U.S. immigration system. The most controversial among these provisions will grant deferred action to as many as 5 million unauthorized aliens.

The President announced the executive actions through ten Department of Homeland Security (DHS) memoranda, two White House memoranda, and three Department of Labor (DOL) fact sheets. Together, they comprise the following initiatives:

- *Border Security:* forming three new task forces as part of DHS's Southern Border and Approaches Campaign Strategy that integrates efforts not only *within* DHS's Customs and Border Protection (CBP) but also among other DHS agencies, such as Immigration and Customs Enforcement (ICE), U.S. Citizenship and Immigration Services (USCIS), and the U.S. Coast Guard;
- *Interior Enforcement and Removals:* revising priorities for immigration enforcement and detention; ending the Secure Communities program and replacing it with the Priority Enforcement Program (PEP), collecting and disseminating improved metrics on removals, and reforming the employment structure for ICE Enforcement and Removal Office (ERO) agents;
- *Expanded Deferred Action for Childhood Arrivals (DACA):* increasing the population eligible for the DACA program by expanding the eligibility criteria, and extending the duration of DACA and its related work authorization from two to three years;
- *Deferred Action for Parents of Americans and Lawful Permanent Residents (DAPA):* allowing parents of U.S. citizens and lawful permanent residents (LPRs) to request deferred action and employment authorization if they meet residency and other criteria and pass required background checks;

- *Parole Rules:* revising conditions under which eligible family members of military personnel, persons traveling abroad, and certain entrepreneurs may receive parole;
- *Provisional Unlawful Presence Waivers:* expanding the use of provisional unlawful presence waivers beyond spouses and minor children of U.S. citizens to also include the spouses and minor children of LPRs as well as the adult children of U.S. citizens, and clarifying the "extreme hardship" standard that must be met to obtain this waiver;
- *High Skilled Workers:* ensuring that all statutorily available LPR visas are fully utilized, reviewing the labor certification program and its regulations to strengthen its integrity and responsiveness to workforce changes, providing foreign workers with greater flexibility to change jobs, expanding the use of national interest waivers to retain selected highly qualified workers, expanding opportunities for students to gain on-the-job training through administrative rule changes, and clarifying the meaning of "specialized knowledge" to ensure U.S. workers are not being unfairly displaced;
- *Immigrant Integration and Naturalization:* initiating an inter-agency task force to identify and promote both immigrant integration "best practices" within states and localities as well as facilitating steps that can be taken administratively within and among federal agencies, and encouraging eligible LPRs to naturalize through additional payment options and possible partial fee waivers;
- *Immigrant Visa System:* providing recommendations to streamline, modernize, and improve immigrant and nonimmigrant visa processing;
- *Labor Protection:* creating an inter-agency working group to promote effective and consistent enforcement of federal labor, employment, and immigration laws to protect all workers regardless of legal status; and
- *Crime Victims:* expanding the DOL Wage and Hour Division's role in supporting foreign national victims of human trafficking and other select crimes.

According to the President, the actions were taken in response to the absence of legislation addressing major problems within the immigration system. The President has stated that his actions are temporary, and that his successor can rescind them. Those opposed to the executive actions argue they were taken largely for political purposes. They contend that once granted, such temporary measures would be difficult to revoke. Separately, a debate has arisen as to whether the President has the legal authority to take such actions, with the Administration and others arguing the President's actions fall within his authority, and many in Congress arguing the President has overstepped it. That debate and its attendant legal questions are beyond the scope of this report.

Because the President announced his executive actions relatively recently, little guidance is available to clarify policies and answer questions related to the revisions and initiatives they include. The two deferred action programs, both of which require petitioners to submit fees, are the only initiatives in the executive action supported by independent fee-supported funding. The rest rely largely on changes in rules and regulations and on the coordination and marshaling of existing administrative resources. As the Administration proceeds to implement the executive actions, some in Congress have vowed to halt some or all of them.

Chapter 4 – This is an edited, reformatted and augmented version of a document issued by the Congressional Budget Office, December 2014.

In: Immigration Policy Proposals ...
Editor: Kimberly D. Parsons
ISBN: 978-1-63482-344-9

Chapter 1

How Changes in Immigration Policy Might Affect the Federal Budget*

Melissa Merrell and Jonathan Schwabish

Summary

During the past two years, the Congress has considered proposals to modify the nation's immigration system. The Border Security, Economic Opportunity, and Immigration Modernization Act (S. 744), passed by the Senate in June 2013, addresses multiple facets of immigration policy, including changes to the existing visa system, improvements in border security and law enforcement, and changes to the status of people who currently live in the country without legal authorization. Other proposals have focused on one component of immigration policy— for example, improving border security or changing certain aspects of the visa system. Whether the proposals involve broad or narrow changes to immigration policy, they could have a variety of consequences for both citizens and noncitizens, for the federal government, and for state and local governments. This Congressional Budget Office (CBO) report examines some of those proposals and how such changes would affect the federal budget.

When estimating the budgetary consequences of immigration reform, CBO considers various factors. Depending on the details of proposed legislation, changes to immigration policy could have a significant effect

* This is an edited, reformatted and augmented version of a report issued by the Congressional Budget Office, January 2015.

on the size and composition of the noncitizen population and, as a result, on rates of participation in federal programs and the payment of taxes. For that reason, when estimating the budgetary effects of proposals, CBO considers the demographic and labor force characteristics of foreign-born people, their eligibility for and participation in federal programs, their tax liability, changes in the economy, and a number of other factors. If proposals were combined into a single, more comprehensive immigration bill, estimates of the budgetary effects would take into account the complex interactions among the various provisions; the net effect would not be a simple summation of the individual effects.

WHAT ARE THE DEMOGRAPHIC AND LABOR FORCE CHARACTERISTICS OF NONCITIZENS?

Of the 41 million foreign-born people living in the United States in 2012, about 22 million were noncitizens—a category that includes lawful permanent residents, or LPRs (people who have been granted permanent admission to the United States and are eligible to live and work here); temporary residents and visitors; and unauthorized residents.[1]

About half of those noncitizens were LPRs, temporary residents, or visitors; the rest, between 11 million and 12 million people, were in the country without authorization, a number that has changed little over the past few years.

Noncitizens differ from both foreign- and native-born citizens across several demographic dimensions, especially in terms of their skills and employment status. In particular, noncitizens are much more likely to be of working age (between 25 and 64 years old) and much less likely to be 65 years old or older.

They are also significantly more likely than citizens to have less than a high school diploma or GED but about as likely to have a master's or more advanced degree, reflecting a broad spectrum of education and skills. Since 1995, the unemployment rate among noncitizens has been, on average, more than a percentage point higher than that for citizens; in 2013, the unemployment rate for noncitizens was 7.1 percent compared with 6.0 percent for citizens.

How Have Recent Administrative Actions Affected Unauthorized Residents?

The Administration has taken a number of steps to delay possible removal proceedings for unauthorized residents under a process known as deferred action. Those who are approved for deferred action are considered lawfully present in the country for a limited period of time but do not gain legal status; they can, and most do, receive authorization to work.

As of September 30, 2014, about 610,000 people who entered the United States as children had been approved for deferred action through the Deferred Action for Childhood Arrivals program. In November 2014, the President expanded that program to include additional people who arrived as children and also established a deferred action program for parents of U.S. citizens and LPRs. CBO estimates that, by 2017, between 2 million and 21/2 million people will have received approval for deferred action.

What Federal Benefits Can Noncitizens Receive and What Taxes Do They Pay?

Under current law, only qualified aliens—primarily comprising LPRs, refugees, and people who have been granted asylum—and some types of temporary residents are eligible to participate in most federal benefit programs, provided they meet other program-specific eligibility requirements. (For some programs, those requirements include waiting periods of several years following the attainment of qualified alien status). Some noncitizens who are not qualified aliens but are lawfully present (for example, people who have been approved for deferred action) are eligible to receive Social Security and Medicare benefits if they qualify on the basis of their age and work history. Other noncitizens are not eligible to receive benefits from most federal programs; exceptions include emergency health care services provided through Medicaid, some benefits through the Children's Health Insurance Program (CHIP), and some refundable tax credits. However, noncitizens' U.S.–born children are eligible for the same federal benefits that are available to other U.S. citizens. (See Table 1 for an overview of the eligibility requirements for noncitizens.)

Most noncitizens who live and work in the United States are subject to taxation—including income taxes, payroll taxes, excise taxes, and estate and gift taxes. The specific taxes for which they are liable, and in some cases the amount of those taxes, depend on the type of visa they hold and how long they have been in the country.

How Might Proposals to Modify the Immigration System Affect the Federal Budget?

Proposals to modify U.S. immigration policy vary greatly in scope and their potential impact on the federal budget. In this report, CBO discusses the possible effects that changes to immigration policy would have on several major federal spending programs and on federal tax revenues. Among the programs and benefits that could be affected:

- Health care programs for low-income people— including Medicaid, CHIP, and subsidies for health insurance (which include premium and cost-sharing assistance for health insurance purchased through the exchanges that were established in 2014 under the Affordable Care Act, or ACA),[2]
- The Supplemental Nutrition Assistance Program (SNAP),
- Social Security,
- Supplemental Security Income (SSI),
- Medicare,
- Pell grants and federal student loans,
- Unemployment insurance, and
- Refundable tax credits.

Each program has its own set of eligibility rules and criteria, which determine how changes to federal immigration policy would affect participation in the program and spending by the government. Consequently, such policy changes could affect spending in varying ways both in the near term and over time. Spending for some programs would change almost immediately upon enactment if more noncitizens were allowed to enter the country, whereas spending for other programs would not change much for a while: For example, under some proposals, foreign-born people who entered the country lawfully after the policy change was implemented would automatically be eligible for emergency Medicaid benefits and subsidies for health insurance purchased through exchanges; they also would begin paying income and payroll taxes as soon as they entered the country. In contrast, additional spending for Social Security and Medicare would occur mostly after the first few decades, once new entrants had been in the workforce for a sufficient time and reached the age at which they were eligible to claim benefits.

Table 1. Noncitizens' Eligibility for Federal Programs

	LPRs, Refugees, and People Granted Asylum	Temporary Residents	Unauthorized Residents
Health Care for Low-Income People			
Medicaid	Only emergency services for the first five years, with some state exceptions for children and pregnant women during those first five years	Emergency services	Emergency services
CHIP	Full coverage for qualified aliens after five years, with some state exceptions for fewer than five years	State option for coverage of prenatal care, labor and delivery, and postpartum care	State option for coverage of prenatal care, labor and delivery, and postpartum care
Premium and cost-sharing assistance[a]	Eligible	Eligible	Not eligible
SNAP	LPRs under the age of 18, refugees, and people granted asylum are immediately eligible; other LPRs must wait five years	Not eligible	Not eligible
Social Security	Eligible	Eligible	Not eligible[b]
SSI	Refugees and people granted asylum are eligible on entrance; LPRs must wait five years and have 40 quarters of work credit	Not eligible	Not eligible
Medicare	Eligible	Eligible	Not eligible[b]

Table 1. (Continued)

	LPRs, Refugees, and People Granted Asylum	Temporary Residents	Unauthorized Residents
Pell Grants and Federal Student Loans	Eligible, no five-year wait	Not eligible	Not eligible
Unemployment Insurance	Eligible	Temporary residents with work authorization only	Not eligible
Refundable Tax Credits	Eligible	Depends on visa, home country, and amount of time in the United States	To receive, a taxpayer must generally fiile his or her tax return and have either a Social Security number or an ITIN.[b]

Source: Congressional Budget Office.

Notes: In addition to those eligibility requirements stated in the table, people must also meet the usual eligibility requirements for each program.

LPR = lawful permanent resident; CHIP = Children's Health Insurance Program; SNAP = Supplemental Nutrition Assistance Program; SSI = Supplemental Security Income; ITIN = individual taxpayer identification number.

[a] Part of the Affordable Care Act, which comprises the Patient Protection and Affordable Care Act (Public Law 111-148) and the health care provisions of the Health Care and Reconciliation Act of 2010 (P.L. 111-152), as affected by subsequent judicial decisions, statutory changes, and administrative actions.

[b] Formerly unauthorized residents who receive approval for "deferred action"—that is, any removal proceedings initiated against them are delayed for a period of time—are considered lawfully present without legal status. They are eligible to receive Medicare and Social Security benefits, assuming they meet the programs' requirements. In addition, unauthorized residents who are approved for deferred action and receive work authorization have Social Security numbers and therefore can claim the earned income tax credit, if they qualify.

Because most noncitizens who live and work in the United States are subject to taxation, changes to federal immigration policy would affect the amount of revenues the government collects. How total revenues collected by the federal government would change under new immigration policy would depend on the resulting changes in the size of the U.S. population, the types of people who would be permitted to work under those new laws, and other considerations. A policy that led to a significant increase in the working-age population would expand the labor force and lead to a significant amount of additional revenues from income and payroll taxes.

This report does not address in detail how a change in immigration policy might affect federal spending or tax revenues through its effects on the broader economy—as evidenced in changes to gross domestic product, employment, and total wages. In some instances, when those effects would probably be significant, CBO and the staff of the Joint Committee on Taxation (JCT) have relaxed the long-standing convention of not incorporating such macroeconomic effects in cost estimates. Immigration legislation also could have a broader set of effects on output and income that are not reflected in cost estimates. Those additional economic effects include changes in the productivity of labor and capital, the income earned by capital, the rate of return on capital (and therefore the interest rate on government debt), and the differences in wages for workers with different skills. Those effects and their estimated consequences for the federal budget have, on occasion, been discussed in separate reports regarding the proposed legislation.

Earlier this month, the House of Representatives adopted a rule that requires CBO and JCT to include the budgetary feedback of any macroeconomic effects in cost estimates for some major pieces of legislation.[3] Legislation that would make significant changes in immigration policy might be covered by this rule; if so, future cost estimates provided to the House for such legislation will, to the extent practicable, incorporate the sorts of effects described here.

Because immigration proposals could affect both spending and revenues, some might result in net budgetary savings whereas others might result in net budgetary costs. However, assessing the net effect on the federal budget of changes in immigration policy is complicated by a variety of factors, including a lack of reliable data about the number of unauthorized residents currently in the country and the extent to which LPRs, temporary residents, and unauthorized residents use government programs. This report focuses on proposals that would change the status or composition of three populations of noncitizens: LPRs, temporary workers, and currently unauthorized residents.

Changing the Criteria for Admitting Lawful Permanent Residents

According to government estimates, about 13 million people currently live in the country as LPRs. Changes to visa policies that broadly affected the characteristics of new LPRs—for example, by shifting the type of permanent visas awarded from family-based preferences to work-related or merit-based preferences— might have a significant impact on the demographic composition of LPRs and, as a result, on their use of federal programs and payment of taxes.

Under current law, permanent residents who meet program requirements are generally eligible to receive benefits after a specified waiting period or period of employment; thus, an increase in the number of LPRs would ultimately increase spending for programs such as Social Security and Medicare. Whether those residents qualify for certain means-tested benefits (such as those provided by Medicaid and SNAP) is determined, in part, by their income. If the policy change resulted in more LPRs with sufficiently low income to qualify for benefits, costs for those federal programs also would increase. In the first five years, the biggest impact on spending would probably involve the health insurance subsidies; after that, changes in spending for other programs would have increased importance. Tax revenues also would change if the visa system was altered, though whether revenues increased or decreased would depend on the details of the policy.

Changes that significantly increased the net flow of foreign-born workers into the United States, and therefore increased the total population, would lead to an increase in the supply of labor, which would have broad effects on the economy and the budget. The magnitude of those effects would depend on factors such as the new immigrants' rate of participation in the labor force, their unemployment rate, the average number of hours they work, and their average wage.

Changing the Visa System for Temporary Workers

The United States issued about 9.2 million visas for temporary admission in 2013. About 670,000 of those visas were issued to temporary workers and the rest were issued to other temporary residents and visitors. Because temporary workers are generally not eligible to receive benefits from most federal programs, policies that changed the number of temporary visas awarded to foreign-born workers might have a smaller effect on the federal budget than changes to the number of permanent residents. However, if a temporary-worker program allowed participants to eventually adjust their status, and the number of LPRs or citizens increased as a result, the long-term fiscal impact of those residents and their children might be significant. A policy that modified the visa system in a way that resulted in a shift in the demographic composition of temporary workers also would affect the federal budget. For example, a shift that resulted in a larger share of people with more skills or education would probably reduce spending on needs-based programs and boost wages and tax revenues.

Granting Legal Status to Unauthorized Residents

Granting legal status to some or all of the noncitizens living in the country without authorization would affect their tax liability, their eligibility for federal benefits, and the amount of benefits they received. Those effects would depend critically on the specific provisions of the legislation, which would determine when and how those newly authorized residents became eligible for federal benefits.

Over time, such changes in status might increase spending for a variety of federal benefits, including those provided by health care programs for low-income people (specifically, Medicaid, CHIP, and subsidies for the purchase of health insurance through the exchanges established by the ACA), SNAP, Social Security, Medicare, and refundable tax credits. Several other federal programs, such as SSI, Pell grants, and unemployment insurance also could experience spending increases.

In addition, legalization policies might result in increased tax revenues, stemming mostly from taxes on higher wages that workers may earn as a result of attaining legal status and taxes from increased reporting of employment income by workers who are currently not paying taxes.

The effects also would vary over time: In the first decade after enactment, the amount that the federal government spent on benefit programs might not rise significantly if waiting periods for benefits remained the same as they are under current law and if other eligibility rules were not changed. In subsequent years, government spending would rise as people crossed those thresholds and became eligible for benefits as they aged (for example, Social Security and Medicare benefits).

In addition, children born in the United States to those residents would be eligible for benefit programs on the same basis as other citizens.

How Might Increased Enforcement of Immigration Law Affect the Federal Budget?

Proposals to enhance the enforcement of immigration law generally focus on improving border security and internal enforcement (the process of identifying, locating, and removing people who entered the country unlawfully or remained after their authorized stay had ended), or on improving the system that allows employers to verify the legal status of new workers.

Bolstering border security and improving internal enforcement could require additional federal funding for personnel—more Border Patrol agents, for instance—or more funding for improved border infrastructure and technologies. Budgetary effects also would include reductions in spending for federal benefit programs and in receipts of tax revenues that stemmed from a decrease in the number of people living in the country without authorization.

Policies designed to improve verification of a person's legal status at the workplace would target the estimated 8 million unauthorized residents who work. Some of those people have received or will receive an authorization to work under the Administration's deferred action authorization, despite requirements for newly hired workers to have evidence of work authorization and identity.

Implementing such proposals might have a significant impact on the federal budget. Expanding the existing E-Verify program would increase administrative costs of the Department of Homeland Security (DHS) and the Social Security Administration (SSA), the agencies responsible for managing the program. Such an expansion might result in lower federal revenues if more unauthorized workers were paid outside of the tax system.

Characteristics of Noncitizens

Over 41 million foreign-born people lived in the United States in 2012, making up about 13 percent of the 314 million U.S. residents that year—the largest share since 1920. Of that foreign-born population, 19 million were naturalized citizens (foreign-born people who have fulfilled the requirements of U.S. citizenship). Twenty-two million were noncitizens (a category that includes foreign-born people authorized to be in the United States, either on a temporary or permanent basis, as well as people who are not authorized to be in the United States). About half of those noncitizens were legally authorized to live or work in the United States.

Foreign-born people can gain legal entry into the United States by qualifying for a temporary stay, such as for work or education, or by qualifying for a permanent stay. They can qualify for a permanent stay by demonstrating a family relationship with a current U.S. citizen or lawful permanent resident, by meeting employment requirements, or by being granted asylum or status as a refugee. Those in the country illegally include people who originally entered without authorization as well as those who remain in the country after such authorization has expired.

Citizens and noncitizens differ in terms of demographics and participation in the labor force. Noncitizens are more likely than citizens to be of working age—between 25 and 64 years old—but they also tend to have less education (see Table 2). Male noncitizens are more likely than male citizens to be in the labor force, but the opposite is true for women. Between 2008 and 2013, the unemployment rate for noncitizen workers between the ages of 25 and 64 was more than a percentage point higher than that for workers who were citizens.

Categories of Noncitizens

The noncitizen population comprises three categories: lawful permanent residents, temporary residents and visitors, and unauthorized residents.[4]

Lawful Permanent Residents

LPRs are granted permanent admission to the United States and receive a document, commonly known as a green card, certifying that status. They are eligible to live and work in the United States, own property, and join the armed forces. Most may apply for U.S. citizenship after five years.[5] In 2013, the United States granted LPR status to 1.0 million people.

Permanent admission can be granted to noncitizens on the basis of any of the following broad criteria:

- Family relationships:
  - Immediate relatives of U.S. citizens—for example, spouses, parents and unmarried children under the age of 21;

- Family-sponsored preferences—for example, married and unmarried sons and daughters of U.S. citizens, spouses and dependent children of LPRs, and siblings of adult U.S. citizens.

o Employment-based preferences—for workers with specific job skills.
o Eligibility for the Diversity Immigrant Visa Program—a lottery-based system for people from countries with low rates of immigration to the United States.
o Humanitarian reasons—for refugees or people who have been granted asylum, who may then apply for LPR status one year later.[6]

In 2013, about two-thirds of the new LPRs received that status on the basis of a family relationship with a U.S. citizen or LPR.

Table 2. Demographic Characteristics of Citizens and Noncitizens, 2012

	Percentage of Total		*Number of People (Millions)*	
	Citizens	*Noncitizens*	*Citizens*	*Noncitizens*
Age Distribution				
Under the age of 25	34	19	101	4
Ages 25 to 64	51	74	150	16
Age 65 or older	15	7	43___	___1
Total	100	100	294	22
Women Currently or Formerly Married[a]				
Ages 15 to 24	8	17	2	*
Ages 25 to 34	53	66	10	2
Educational Attainment, Ages 25 to 64				
Less than high school diploma or GED	9	39	13	6
High school diploma or GED	27	23	40	4
Some college or associate's degree	32	15	48	2
Bachelor's degree	21	13	31	2
Master's degree or more	11	10	17___	___2
Total	101	99	150	16
Labor Force Participation Rate, Ages 25 to 64				
Men	82	89	61 [b]	7 b
Women	73	60	56 [b]_____	___5[b]
Total	78	75	116 b	12 b

	Percentage of Total		*Number of People (Millions)*	
	Citizens	*Noncitizens*	*Citizens*	*Noncitizens*
Total	93	7	294	22
Memorandum:				
Fertililty Rates of Women, Ages 15 to 49[c]	1.8	2.3	n.a.	n.a.
Median Earnings in 2010, Ages 25 to 64 (Dollars)[d]				
Male Workers	45,000	26,000	n.a.	n.a.
Female Workers	31,700	18,200	n.a.	n.a.
All Workers	38,000	23,400	n.a.	n.a.

Source: Congressional Budget Office based on data from the Census Bureau.

Notes: Demographic information presented here is based on data from the Census Bureau's 2013 American Community Survey as extracted from the Minnesota Population Center's Integrated Public Use Microdata Series. Unemployment information is based on data from outgoing rotation groups of the Census Bureau's monthly Current Population Survey, January 1994 to December 2013.

* = less than 500,000; n.a. = not applicable.

[a] Consists of all women who are married, divorced, separated, or widowed.

[b] Refers to the number of people participating in the labor force.

[c] The expected number of births experienced by a woman in a particular age range if, at each age within the range, the likelihood that she gave birth was equal to the share of women at the same age who bore a child during the survey year.

[d] Calculated for individuals between the ages of 25 and 64 with positive earnings.

Temporary Residents and Visitors

Temporary admission to the United States is granted to foreign-born people who seek entry for a limited time and for a specific purpose, such as tourism, diplomacy, or study. In addition, people may be permitted into the United States to work for a limited time. Foreign-born people with temporary visas are generally not eligible for citizenship, and to remain in the United States on a permanent basis they would be required to apply for permanent admission.

The United States issued about 9.2 million visas for temporary admission in 2013, 58 percent more than the number issued in 2009. Visitors accounted for 81 percent of those visas; about 12 percent were issued to temporary residents such as students and their families; and temporary workers and their families accounted for about 7 percent. Much of the increase was attributable to tourist visas, perhaps because the global recession had begun to moderate by 2012.[7]

Unauthorized Residents

DHS estimates that between 11 million and 12 million U.S. residents were in the country without authorization in 2012.[8] Unauthorized residents either enter the country illegally or stay beyond the time allowed by a visa. Nearly half of the unauthorized residents in the U.S. are believed to have originally entered the country legally.[9] The estimates suggest that the total number of unauthorized residents has risen by about 3 million since 2000. Some unauthorized residents have been approved for deferred action (see Box 1). Those residents are lawfully present without legal status.

Demographic Characteristics of Noncitizens

As a group, noncitizens differ in several important ways from citizens—whether naturalized or native born—in terms of age, marital status, fertility, and educational attainment. Those characteristics in part determine citizens' and noncitizens' eligibility for and participation in certain government programs. Therefore, such information, including when noncitizens become citizens, is important to CBO's estimates of the budgetary effects of immigration policy proposals.[10]

Age

Compared with the citizen population, a relatively small share of noncitizens are under the age of 25 or over 65. In 2012, about one-fifth of the noncitizen population was under age 25, compared with about one-third of the citizen population (see Table 2 on page 7). In that year, only 7 percent of noncitizens were at least 65 years old, less than half the share among citizens. In contrast, nearly three-quarters of the noncitizen population was of working age (between 25 and 64 years old), compared with about half of the citizen population. According to DHS, most of the unauthorized residents were between 25 and 54 years old in 2012—about three-quarters of the unauthorized population were in that age group, compared with about half of citizens.[11]

Box 1. Unauthorized Residents and Deferred Action

In some cases, the Department of Homeland Security (DHS) delays removal proceedings for unauthorized residents under a process known as deferred action.

Those who are approved for deferred action are considered lawfully present in the country but do not gain legal status. They can, and most do, receive authorization to work. Because they are lawfully present during the period of their deferred status, they are eligible to receive Medicare and Social Security benefits if they meet the programs' requirements. In addition, those individuals who are approved for deferred action and receive work authorization have Social Security numbers and therefore can claim the earned income tax credit if they qualify. They are ineligible for other federal benefit programs.

Childhood Arrivals. In August 2012, DHS began accepting and processing applications for deferred action from some unauthorized residents who did not yet have removal proceedings initiated against them. To qualify for this program, known as the Deferred Action for Childhood Arrivals (DACA) program, people had to meet several requirements: they must have been under 31 years of age as of June 15, 2012; been younger than 16 when they came to the United States; continuously resided in the United States since June 15, 2007; been registered in and attending school, or have graduated from high school or earned a GED; or had been honorably discharged from the military. Deferred action was granted for two years and could be renewed. The Migration Policy Institute estimates that about 2.1 million unauthorized residents may be eligible for DACA as implemented since 2012.[1] As of September 30, 2014, DHS had received about 700,000 initial applications and approved about 630,000 requests, including about 22,000 renewals of status.[2]

On November 20, 2014, the President announced a series of changes to immigration policy, including expanding DACA.[3] That executive action expands the DACA population in two ways. It allows people who are 31 years and older and arrived in the United States as children, and unauthorized residents who meet the other DACA requirements but who arrived between June 15, 2007, and January 1, 2010, to apply for deferred action. Those two groups were excluded from the original DACA program.

In addition, the November action extended the duration of deferred action from two years under previous Administration policy to three years.

The Congressional Budget Office (CBO) estimates that in 2017 there will be about 600,000 people in the country approved for deferred action as a result of the initial DACA program and about another 150,000 people approved for deferred action as a result of the expanded eligibility.

Parents of U.S. Citizens and Lawful Permanent Residents. The executive actions announced on November 20, 2014, also allow parents of U.S. citizens and lawful permanent residents to apply for deferred action if they meet the following criteria: they have been continuously present in the country since January 1, 2010; were physically present in the country on November 20, 2014, and at the time of application; had no legal status on November 20, 2014; and are not an enforcement priority for DHS. CBO estimates that in 2017 there will be about 1.5 million parents of U.S. citizens or lawful permanent residents in the country approved for deferred action as a result of the new policy.

[1]. Jeanne Batalova, Sarah Hooker, and Randy Capps, DACA at the Two-Year Mark: A National and State Profile of Youth Eligible and Applying for Deferred Action (Migration Policy Institute, August 2014), http://tinyurl.com/nq6kapo (PDF, 4.92 MB).

[2] Citizenship and Immigration Services, "Consideration of Deferred Action for Childhood Arrivals, by Fiscal Year, Quarter, Intake, Biometrics, and Case Status, 2012 to 2014" (November 21, 2014), http://go.usa.gov/eWrk(PDF, 131 KB).

[3] Jeh Charles Johnson, Secretary, Department of Homeland Security, memorandum about exercising prosecutorial discretion with respect to individuals who came to the United States as children and with respect to certain individuals who are the parents of U.S. citizens or permanent residents (November 20, 2014), http://go.usa.gov/eWrz (PDF, 3 MB).

Marital Status and Fertility

Marriage and fertility rates are generally higher among young female noncitizens than among their citizen counterparts. In 2012, 17 percent of female noncitizens ages 15 to 24 were or had been married, roughly double the share of female citizens; about two-thirds of female noncitizens ages 25 to 34 were or had been married, compared with just over half of female citizens. (The available data do not permit a reliable estimate of the percentage of marriages in which one spouse is an unauthorized resident.) The fertility rate— the expected number of births—among female noncitizens between the ages of 15 and 49 was 2.3, compared with a fertility rate of 1.8 for female citizens in the same age range.

Educational Attainment

Noncitizens' educational attainment also differs considerably from that of citizens. In 2012, about 40 percent of the noncitizen population between the ages of 25 and 64 had less than a high school diploma or GED, more than four times the share of the citizen population. A similar share of citizens and noncitizens had a high school diploma or GED, but citizens were much more likely than noncitizens to have at least some college education (64 percent compared with 38 percent).

Labor Market Characteristics of Noncitizens

Male noncitizens are more likely, and female noncitizens less likely, than their citizen counterparts to be in the labor force. Overall, the unemployment rate for non-citizens tends to be higher than for citizens, and earnings for noncitizens tend to be lower.

Labor Force Participation

In 2012, a slightly greater share of citizens ages 25 to 64 participated in the labor force than did noncitizens in that age group, but there were significant differences between men and women. In that year, the labor force participation rate among male noncitizens was about 7 percentage points higher than among male citizens. By contrast, the labor force participation rate among female noncitizens was about 13 percentage points lower than among female citizens.[12]

Unemployment Rate

Unemployment rates vary over time with economic conditions. Nevertheless, over the past two decades, the unemployment rate has been consistently higher for noncitizen workers than it has been for citizen workers (see Figure 1). During that period, economic fluctuations resulted in larger changes in the unemployment rate among noncitizens than among citizens. The unemployment rate for noncitizens declined more than that for citizens between 1995 and 2000 and again between 2003 and 2006, when the economy was growing quickly. Conversely, the unemployment rate for noncitizen workers rose more than the rate for citizen workers between 2000 and 2003, when the economy was shrinking or growing slowly. And between 2006 and 2010, the unemployment rate among noncitizen workers between the ages of 25 and 64 rose by about 5.7 percentage points—from 4.2 percent to 9.9 percent—compared with a 4.6 percentage-point increase among citizen workers.

At least four factors contributed to the changes in employment experienced by noncitizens in recent years: a disproportionate decrease in employment in the construction sector because of the decline in the housing market; the fact that job losses among those with less education occurred at a faster rate than was the case for people with greater educational attainment; variations in local labor markets resulting from changes in demand for certain kinds of jobs; and changes in the number and types of noncitizens in the country.

Since the end of the recent recession, the gap between the unemployment rates has narrowed, but it is still larger than it was before the recession. For citizens, the unemployment rate declined from 8.2 percent in 2010 to 6.0 percent in 2013. Among the noncitizen population, the unemployment rate fell from 9.9 percent in 2010 to 7.1 percent in 2013.

Annual Earnings

Disparities between the annual earnings of noncitizen and citizen workers can be attributed to differences in age, educational attainment, labor force participation, and the concentration of workers in particular occupational groups. In 2012, median earnings among male citizens were about 75 percent greater than those of male noncitizens; female citizens also earned about 75 percent more than their noncitizen counterparts.

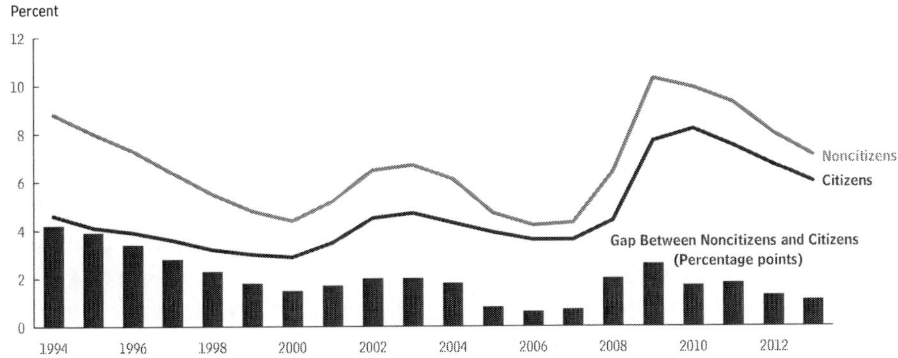

Source: Congressional Budget Office based on data from outgoing rotation groups of the Census Bureau's monthly Current Population Survey, January 1994 to December 2013, www.census.gov/cps.

Figure 1. Unemployment Rates Among Citizens and Noncitizens Ages 25 to 64, 1994 to 2013.

Noncitizens' Eligibility for Federal Benefits and Their Tax Liability

Changes to federal immigration policy would affect the number of people eligible for federal benefits, the number of beneficiaries who participate in a variety of federal programs, and the amount of taxes people pay. Such changes might occur through policies that modified the current visa system and altered the number of people legally admitted to the country or policies that offered unauthorized residents legal status.

Under current law, only certain noncitizens referred to collectively as qualified aliens—primarily LPRs, refugees, and people who have been granted asylum—are eligible for many public benefit programs.[13] (Most other types of noncitizens—temporary workers, visitors, and all unauthorized residents—are not considered qualified aliens.) Such eligibility restrictions are not universal, however; all noncitizens, for example, may receive emergency Medicaid benefits.

Because U.S.–born children of noncitizens are themselves citizens, and thus may be eligible for federal benefits not available to their parents, their participation in various programs also affects the federal budget. Their status as citizens may entitle them to receive benefits through Medicaid, SNAP, SSI, and other such programs. In the future, as those citizen-children age and enter the labor force, they will be liable for taxes and ultimately eligible for Social Security and Medicare benefits on their own behalf.

This section provides an overview of the federal benefit programs that would most likely be affected by changes to immigration policy. In addition, it explores how such policy changes would affect federal tax revenues.

The budgetary effects of changes to immigration policy would vary over time. Many of the federal programs discussed in this report limit eligibility or require waiting periods before noncitizens are eligible to receive benefits (see Table 1 on page 3). Future immigration policies that raised immigration rates or changed the immigration status of current noncitizen residents, but left those waiting periods unchanged, would probably have relatively small effects on federal spending over the first five years (the current waiting period for several programs). Thereafter, changes to immigration policy would have larger effects, as more residents became eligible for some programs (such as Medicaid) or grew older and qualified for other programs (such as Social Security and Medicare). However, spending might not change in proportion to the number of people granted eligibility because noncitizens tend to have lower income than citizens and, for a variety of reasons, some people choose not to claim benefits for which they are eligible.

Federal Benefits

Changes to immigration policy could have wide-ranging effects on major federal benefit programs: health care programs for low-income people, SNAP, Social Security, SSI, Medicare, Pell grants, federal student loans, and unemployment insurance. Absent changes in eligibility requirements, the largest costs to the federal government, especially in the first decade, would probably result from additional spending for health care.

In general, noncitizens who might be eligible for many of the major federal spending programs have slightly lower participation rates in those programs than do citizens.[14] It is unclear from the available data, however, whether differences in participation rates were attributable to differences in eligibility, the degree to which eligible people participate in a benefit program, or some combination of the two.[15]

Health Care Programs for Low-Income People

Health care programs for people with low income include Medicaid, CHIP, and the health insurance subsidies (including premium and cost-sharing assistance) that became available through exchanges beginning in 2014 under the Affordable Care Act. Noncitizens' eligibility for Medicaid and CHIP benefits is limited, but most lawfully present noncitizens can receive insurance subsidies if they meet the qualifications set in the ACA.

Medicaid and CHIP. Medicaid and CHIP are joint federal-state programs that pay for health care services for a variety of low-income people. Most children and pregnant women in low-income families can qualify for Medicaid or CHIP if they are citizens. In addition, some parents of those children also qualify for Medicaid, although the income thresholds vary by state.[16] As a result of the ACA, some nonelderly people with income below 138 percent of the FPL have become eligible for Medicaid starting in 2014.[17] Those new beneficiaries consist primarily of nonelderly adults with low income who are not parents of dependent children.

Medicaid coverage for noncitizens who are not qualified aliens is limited to emergency services; that limitation also applies in most cases during the first five years after an individual becomes a qualified alien. In 2010, about 1.7 million people received such emergency Medicaid benefits at an average cost to the federal government of about $1,100 per person. Under CHIP, states have the option to provide coverage for prenatal care, labor and delivery, and postpartum care to low-income women regardless of their immigration status. As of January 2013, 15 states had opted to do so.

In addition, since 2009, states have had the option to use federal matching funds to provide coverage through Medicaid, CHIP, or both to children and to pregnant women during the first five years after they become a qualified alien. As of January 2013, 25 states and the District of Columbia had exercised that option.

After any person has been a qualified alien for five years, states have the option of providing full Medicaid and CHIP benefits if the person meets the other eligibility criteria for the program—and all states have chosen to do so.[18]

Health Insurance Subsidies. The ACA established health insurance exchanges through which certain individuals and families may be eligible for tax credits for premium assistance and reduced cost sharing. For some people, those subsidies substantially reduce the cost of purchasing health insurance. Most people who are in the country legally but lack access to certain other sources of coverage—including Medicaid, CHIP, and affordable employment-based insurance—are eligible for those subsidies if they meet income and certain other requirements. To be eligible for premium assistance credits, a household has to have income between 100 percent and 400 percent of the FPL, and the amount of the credit depends on the cost of the health insurance plan and the person's income. Further, people who are lawfully present and whose income is less than 100 percent of the FPL, but who are ineligible for Medicaid because of their immigration status, are eligible for exchange subsidies as long as they meet other eligibility requirements.[19] Unauthorized residents are not eligible to receive health insurance subsidies.

Supplemental Nutrition Assistance Program

SNAP provides benefits to help people in low-income households purchase food. Eligibility for SNAP is generally based on the income and assets of members of the household or on the participation of household members in other assistance programs.[20]

Unauthorized residents and temporary residents are not eligible for benefits. For LPRs and refugees to qualify, they must meet specific requirements in addition to the usual eligibility criteria. For example, most adult LPRs must wait five years, whereas LPRs under the age of 18 can receive benefits at any point. (Some noncitizens, such as refugees and those granted asylum, are eligible for benefits without a waiting period.)

Social Security

The federal government's largest program in terms of spending, Social Security provides benefits to retired workers (through Old-Age and Survivors Insurance), to people with disabilities (through Disability Insurance, or DI), and to their families, as well as to some survivors of deceased workers. Those benefits are financed primarily by payroll taxes collected on people's earnings. To qualify for retirement benefits, workers must meet a "quarters of coverage" criterion that essentially requires them to have worked in the United States for one-fourth (40 quarters) of their adult life. For younger people with disabilities, fewer quarters are required.[21]

The Social Security program does not impose a citizenship requirement; for example, noncitizens such as LPRs and refugees who meet the program's qualifications may receive benefits.[22] However, Social Security benefits may not be paid to people who are not lawfully present in the United States or who do not live in a specific group of foreign countries in which they may receive benefits.[23]

Supplemental Security Income

SSI provides cash benefits to people with low income and few assets who are disabled, elderly (age 65 or over), or both. The program uses the same medical criteria for adults as those used for DI benefits. All states provide Medicaid coverage for SSI beneficiaries, but some states have more restrictive eligibility requirements than others.[24]

Aside from refugees, people who have been granted asylum, and certain others admitted on humanitarian grounds, noncitizens who entered the United States after 1996 must naturalize or obtain 40 quarters (10 years) of work credit and spend five years as lawful permanent residents to become eligible for the SSI program. In the case of their noncitizen children, eligibility is based on the parents' quarters of work credit. Thus, obtaining SSI benefits is more difficult than qualifying for DI benefits. (DI has less stringent quarters-of-coverage requirements and only requires that the recipient be lawfully present in the country.) Unauthorized residents cannot receive SSI benefits under any circumstances.

Medicare

The Medicare. program provides subsidized medical insurance to the elderly and to some people with disabilities. People generally become eligible for Medicare at age 65 (if they have worked long enough to qualify for Social Security retirement benefits) or two years after they qualify for Social Security DI benefits.

As with the Social Security program, Medicare does not impose a citizenship requirement: LPRs, refugees, and people who have been granted asylum may receive benefits if they meet the program's qualifications. Lawfully present noncitizens who do not meet the program's work requirements but who have been LPRs for at least five years can enroll in both Medicare Parts A (Hospital Insurance) and B (Medical Insurance) but must pay premiums to receive benefits. They may also enroll in Part D (prescription drug coverage) if they have also enrolled in both Parts A and B.

People who are not lawfully present in the United States are ineligible to receive Medicare benefits. In addition, Medicare does not provide coverage outside of the United States. Thus, people who work in the United States and pay Medicare taxes but relocate to another country when they are eligible for Medicare benefits do not receive coverage.

Pell Grants and Federal Student Loans

The federal government operates a number of different programs to help students pay for tuition, books, and living expenses at postsecondary institutions. To qualify for federal student aid, such as Pell grants or federal student loans, students who are noncitizens must meet several requirements. In terms of status, they must be one of the following: an LPR; a conditional permanent resident (a noncitizen who gains entrance to the United States because he or she has married a U.S. citizen or an LPR, or has invested in a U.S. business); a refugee; an individual who has been granted asylum; or someone who falls in one of certain other eligible categories of noncitizens.[25] In addition, they must be enrolled in or accepted for enrollment as a regular student in an eligible degree or certificate program; and for Pell grants and subsidized student loans, they must demonstrate financial need.[26] Unlike most other federal benefit programs, it is not necessary to wait at least five years to qualify for Pell grants and federal student loans.

Unemployment Insurance

The unemployment insurance program provides benefits to workers who have become unemployed through no fault of their own and who meet specified criteria. A number of factors determine whether an individual is eligible for unemployment insurance. For example, to qualify for minimum benefits, the worker must have sufficient work history (as specified by state law) in an occupation covered by the Federal Unemployment Tax Act. In addition, an individual who files for benefits must be actively seeking work. As a result, only a fraction of unemployed people collect unemployment benefits.[27]

Noncitizens who work in the country with legal authorization—including LPRs and some temporary workers— are eligible for unemployment insurance benefits if they meet established criteria when they become unemployed.[28]

Additional rules specify that the noncitizen worker must still be eligible to work in the United States when he or she receives benefits. Unauthorized workers—including those who are unlawfully present and those who are lawfully present but not authorized to work in the United States—are ineligible for unemployment insurance benefits.[29]

Refundable Tax Credits

Depending on circumstances and an individual's income, the Internal Revenue Service (IRS) may make a payment, in the form of a refundable tax credit, to a person that exceeds his or her tax liability.[30] In addition to the tax credits for health insurance premiums mentioned above, other examples include the earned income tax credit (EITC) and the child tax credit.

To receive a refundable tax credit, an individual generally must file his or her tax return with the IRS, have either a Social Security number or an individual taxpayer identification number (ITIN), and meet various other requirements, depending on the specific credit. Of the existing credits, the EITC has the most stringent requirement for noncitizens. To receive the EITC, the recipient, his or her spouse, and the child or children generally must have a Social Security number that is valid for employment in the United States.[31] Those requirements make it difficult for unauthorized residents to receive the EITC. Criteria for receiving the child tax credit are less strict than those for the EITC, but the child must be a citizen or resident of the United States, and both the child and the filer must have a Social Security number or an ITIN.[32]

Tax Liability

Noncitizens who live and work in the United States are liable for some taxes, and changes in their status or changes in the flow of people entering and leaving the country would affect federal revenues as well as outlays. The extent to which revenues increased or decreased would vary depending on the specifics of the legislation and on the type of tax.

All taxpayers whose income exceeds a certain threshold are required to file a tax return and, if their income is greater than a second threshold, they must pay individual income taxes. If they are employed, income taxes on their earnings are withheld during the year by their employer. Social insurance, or payroll, taxes are also withheld from earnings by employers in full each pay period. Self-employed people generally pay estimated taxes (including both income and social insurance taxes) quarterly. Other federal taxes for which noncitizens may be responsible include excise taxes, estate taxes, and gift taxes.

Changes in federal revenues resulting from changes in immigration policy would depend on whether the policy altered the legal status and number of new or existing residents. If the flow of noncitizens into the country increased, for example, federal revenues would rise when those individuals began to work and pay taxes. If a policy modified the immigration status of unauthorized residents currently living in the country, federal tax revenues also might increase, but the effect on revenues would depend on the way the policy was structured, the extent to which those workers currently pay taxes, and whether the change in their status led to an increase in their earnings.[33] Two studies have estimated that at least half of unauthorized residents already pay income and payroll taxes.[34]

PROPOSALS THAT WOULD CHANGE NONCITIZENS' STATUS

Over the past decade, the Congress has considered a variety of proposals that would change the number, type, and legal status of noncitizens in the United States. Certain proposals would modify the visa system for permanent residents and temporary workers and grant legal residency to some or most of the residents currently in the country without authorization. The proposed changes vary greatly in scope and could affect many federal programs and thus have significant effects on the federal budget. Although this report focuses largely on the spending side of the federal budget, changes to immigration policies also could have a significant effect on tax revenues. Some of those proposals would result in net budgetary savings whereas others would result in net budgetary costs.

This report does not address in detail how a change in immigration policy might affect federal spending or tax revenues through its effects on the broader economy—as evidenced in changes to gross domestic product, employment, and total wages. In some instances, when those effects would probably be significant, CBO and JCT have relaxed the long-standing convention of not incorporating such macroeconomic effects in cost estimates (see Box 2).[35] Immigration legislation also could have a broader set of effects on output and income that have not been reflected in cost estimates. Those additional economic effects include changes in the productivity of labor and capital, the income earned by capital, the rate of return on capital (and therefore the interest rate on government debt), and the differences in wages for workers with different skills. Those effects and their estimated consequences for the federal budget have, on occasion, been discussed in separate reports regarding the proposed legislation.[36]

Earlier this month, the House of Representatives adopted a rule that requires CBO and JCT to include the budgetary feedback of any macroeconomic effects in cost estimates for some major pieces of legislation.[37] Legislation that would make significant changes in immigration policy might be covered by this rule; if so, future cost estimates provided to the House for such legislation will, to the extent practicable, incorporate the sorts of effects described here.

Changing the Criteria for Admitting Lawful Permanent Residents

To enter the United States as an LPR or as a temporary resident, a person must obtain a visa from the Department of State and the Department of Homeland Security. To qualify for permanent admission (that is, as an LPR), a foreign-born person must be one of the following: an immediate relative of a U.S. citizen; eligible for family-sponsored preferences; eligible for employment-based preferences; the holder of a diversity program visa; a refugee or a person granted asylum; or someone who meets certain other criteria. According to data from the State Department, the United States granted LPR status to about 1.0 million people in 2013. The wait time varies significantly for both family-sponsored and employment visas. For most categories of family-sponsored visas, the wait time is more than half a decade and for some people it can be more than two decades. For most employment visas, the current wait time is one year or less, although for skilled or professional workers from China and India, the wait time can be almost 10 years or more.[38]

Policies that broadly affected the characteristics of new LPRs—for instance, by shifting permanent visas from a family-based system to a merit-based system that gave priority to workers with particular skills—could have a significant impact on the average educational attainment of LPRs and, as a result, on their average income, earnings, tax payments, and use of federal programs. The Border Security, Economic Opportunity, and Immigration

Modernization Act, for example, would establish a point system to determine which applicants received a visa.[39] Alternatively, an independent commission could assess demand from employers each year and determine the number and type of work visas to allocate.[40]

Factors CBO Considers When Estimating the Budgetary Effects of Legislation

The current visa system could be modified in a number of ways. How the policy changed the number and characteristics of people eligible to become LPRs would have implications for federal spending and revenues. Among the issues CBO would consider when estimating the effects of such policy proposals are the following:

- Would the total number of people entering the country with a visa increase, decrease, or remain roughly unchanged?
- Would the visa system shift from its current emphasis on family-based immigration to a system that favored skill- or employment-based immigration?
- How would limits on types of visas be determined, and how often would those limits change?
- What percentage of potential LPRs would be new entrants, and what percentage would already be in the country and adjusting status?

Effects on Federal Spending and Revenues

Changes to the existing visa system for permanent residents could have significant effects on the U.S. economy and on the federal budget. The direction and magnitude of those effects would depend on whether the policies increased or decreased the total number of LPRs and how the policies affected the demographic makeup of that population. Under current law, permanent residents who meet program requirements are generally eligible to receive benefits after a specified waiting period or period of employment; thus, an increase in the number of LPRs would ultimately increase spending for programs such as Social Security and Medicare. Whether those residents qualify for certain means-tested benefits (such as those provided by Medicaid and SNAP) is determined, in part, by their income.

Box 2. Macroeconomic Effects of Changes in Immigration Policy

Following the long-standing convention of not incorporating macroeconomic effects in cost estimates—a practice that has been followed in the Congressional budget process since it was established in 1974—cost estimates produced by the Congressional Budget Office (CBO) and by the staff of the Joint Committee on Taxation (JCT) typically reflect the assumption that macroeconomic variables such as gross domestic product (GDP) and employment remain fixed at the values they are projected to reach under current law. Thus, when estimating the potential effects of legislative proposals on the federal budget, CBO and JCT generally assume that before-tax wages, the labor supply, and other characteristics of the overall economy would not change as a result of the legislation. (In most cases, those effects would be negligible.) This convention has been followed in estimating the costs of legislation that would make small changes to immigration policy. A change in immigration policy that substantially increased the total population of the United States, however, would cause significant changes in the labor force that were a direct consequence and fundamental objective of the legislation. The magnitude of those changes would depend on the net change in immigration under the policy, as well as how such factors as labor force participation, unemployment rates, average hours of work, and average wages would differ under the policy in comparison with CBO's baseline projections.[1]

In such cases, CBO and JCT have relaxed the standard assumption of not accounting for macroeconomic effects of legislation. An example is the cost estimate for S. 744, the Border Security, Economic Opportunity, and Immigration Modernization Act, as reported by the Senate Judiciary Committee in June 2013. That bill would have significantly increased the size of the U.S. labor force: Relative to CBO's projections under then-current law, enacting that version of S. 744 would have increased the size of the labor force by about 6 million (about 3.5 percent) in 2023 and by about 9 million (about 5 percent) in 2033, CBO and JCT estimated. Employment would have been expected to increase as the labor force expanded because many of the additional immigrants would seek jobs and the larger population would boost demand for goods and services and, in turn, the demand for labor.

But following the standard convention of assuming that employment would remain unchanged relative to current law would have implied that any employment of the additional immigrants would be offset one-for-one by lower employment elsewhere in the population. Because that outcome would be highly implausible, CBO and JCT relaxed the assumption of fixed GDP and employment and incorporated into the cost estimate their projections of the legislation's direct effects on the U.S. population, employment, and taxable compensation, which primarily affected the amount of additional tax revenues that would have resulted from enacting the bill. Nevertheless, to remain as consistent as possible with the estimating rules that CBO and JCT follow for almost all other legislation, the cost estimate for S. 744 did not incorporate the budgetary impact of every economic consequence of the bill. Rather, in a separate report that accompanied the cost estimate, CBO described the effects that were not taken into account in that estimate (specifically, changes in the productivity of labor and capital, the income earned by capital, the rate of return on capital—and therefore the interest rate on government debt and the differences in wages for workers with different skills) and the additional budgetary effects that would ensue.[2] CBO and JCT have anticipated taking a similar approach for any future legislation that would make major changes in immigration policy—reflecting any significant changes in the size of the U.S. population and labor force in the cost estimate for the bill and describing any broader macroeconomic effects in supplemental material. However, earlier this month, the House of Representatives adopted a rule that requires CBO and JCT to include the budgetary feedback of any macroeconomic effects in cost estimates for some major pieces of legislation.[3] Legislation that would make significant changes in immigration policy might be covered by this rule; if so, future cost estimates provided to the House for such legislation will, to the extent practicable, incorporate both the direct effects of changes in the size of the U.S. population and labor force under the bill and any broader macroeconomic effects of the bill.

[1] CBO's baseline projections are not intended to be a prediction of future budgetary outcomes; rather, they serve as a neutral benchmark that lawmakers can use to measure the potential effects of tax and spending proposals.

[2] See Congressional Budget Office, The Economic Impact of S. 744, the Border Security, Economic Opportunity, and Immigration Modernization Act (June 2013), www.cbo.gov/ publication/44346.

[3] See section 2(c) of H. Res. 5, adopted on January 6, 2015, which added clause 8 to Rule XIII

If the policy change resulted in more LPRs with sufficiently low income to qualify for benefits, costs for those federal programs also would increase. In the first five years, the biggest effect on spending would probably involve the health insurance subsidies established by the ACA; after that, changes in spending for other programs would have increased importance. Tax revenues also would change if the visa system was altered, although whether revenues increased or decreased would depend on the details of the policy. Proposals that changed existing criteria for issuing visas or created new categories of visas tailored to specific groups of people, but that did not change the overall number or characteristics of new LPRs, would probably have little effect on federal programs.

Health Care Programs for Low-Income People, SNAP, and SSI

Proposals that increased the number of permanent residents eligible for benefits from means-tested programs, such as Medicaid, CHIP, subsidies for health insurance obtained through exchanges, SNAP, and SSI, would increase federal expenditures on those programs. Under the programs' current requirements, most people would be subject to a waiting period before receiving benefits. (The exchange subsidies do not require a waiting period, however.) Conversely, changes to the visa system that reduced the number of eligible beneficiaries would result in lower expenditures than are projected under current law.

Social Security and Medicare

Proposals that increased the number of LPRs would result in greater federal spending for Social Security and Medicare. In the short term, few of those LPRs would qualify for Social Security and Medicare on the basis of age or disability (although, under current law, people can qualify for Social Security disability benefits—and consequently Medicare—and for Social Security survivors' benefits with fewer than 10 years of covered employment). In the long term, federal spending would increase significantly as those people got older and were more susceptible to a disability or reached their retirement age. A reduction in the number of LPRs would have the opposite effect.

Pell Grants and Federal Student Loans

LPRs can qualify for Pell grants and student loans if they meet the standard eligibility criteria that apply to all recipients. Policies that increased the number of permanent residents would probably result in greater federal spending on those grants and an increase in the volume of student loans.

Unemployment Insurance

Under current law, LPRs qualify for unemployment insurance if they meet the regular eligibility rules. A policy that increased the number of permanent residents would result in a larger workforce. Hence, the number of unemployed at a given unemployment rate would be greater and expenditures for unemployment insurance would be higher.

Refundable Tax Credits, Income Taxes, and Payroll Taxes

Aggregate changes in taxes stemming from policies that changed the number of LPRs in the country would depend on how a change to immigration policy altered the demographic makeup of the population and on the direction and magnitude of those effects. A policy that resulted in an increase in the number of permanent residents at all earnings levels would result in higher total revenues and more spending for refundable tax credits, but the net effect would depend on the specific provisions of the legislation. Policies that favored permanent residents with higher income and reduced the number of permanent residents with lower income would increase revenue from federal income and payroll taxes and decrease spending for refundable tax credits. Conversely, changes to the visa system that increased the number of permanent residents with lower earnings and reduced the number with higher earnings would result in lower revenues from income and payroll taxes and greater spending for refundable tax credits.

Changing the Visa System for Temporary Workers

In the past, the Congress has considered proposals that would increase the number and types of temporary workers in the country without instituting changes to other parts of the visa system. Increases in the number of temporary workers could significantly affect the U.S. economy through, for example, changes in gross domestic product, employment, and total wages. However, such increases would have a smaller impact on the federal budget than increases in the number of permanent residents because temporary workers (like other temporary residents and visitors) generally are ineligible to receive most benefits.

Under current law, temporary visas are available for high-skilled and low-skilled workers. According to data from the State Department, the United States issued about 670,000 temporary visas to temporary workers and their families in 2013.[41]

Many people who are admitted to the United States as temporary workers enter with what is called an H-1B visa. H-1B visas are awarded to workers with "distinguished merit and ability performing services other than a registered nurse." About 153,000 visas of this type were issued in 2013, up from about 111,000 in 2009. Because workers with H-1B visas typically have higher earnings than other foreign-born workers, policies that increased the number of H-1B workers in the country would probably have little impact on federal spending in the short term but would increase tax revenues.[42] Policies that increased the number of H-1B workers while decreasing the number of visas for new permanent residents would probably result in reduced spending on need-based programs in the short-term.

Coupled with increased border security and internal enforcement efforts, programs that expanded opportunities for both high-skilled and low-skilled temporary workers could result in a net decrease in the number of unauthorized residents in the country; but the effects of such policy changes would go in both directions. On the one hand, people who might otherwise have entered the country illegally might choose to enter through temporary-worker programs. On the other hand, expanded temporary-worker programs might result in an increase in the number of unauthorized residents if those workers overstayed (that is, remained in the country after their authorization has expired). Increased border security and internal enforcement, however, would result in the removal of some people who overstayed and have the additional effect of reducing the number of other unauthorized residents in the country.

In analyzing changes to the visa system for temporary workers, CBO might anticipate the following:

- A substantial number of people would apply for an expanded number of temporary-worker visas because of employers' demand for workers who can enter the country legally and because workers from other countries tend to seek higher-paying jobs in the United States;
- At least within the first few years of a policy's enactment, some workers who applied for such visas would be new entrants who would

not otherwise have entered the United States, whereas others would have entered the country without authorization;

- Many of those workers would extend their temporary visas and become LPRs if such options were made available as part of a policy granting more temporary-worker visas; and
- Some of the additional temporary workers would overstay their visas and become unauthorized residents. It is unclear, however, whether the demographic and economic characteristics of those unauthorized residents—and thus their rates of eligibility for various federal programs—would be similar to those of the unauthorized residents currently living in the country.

Factors CBO Considers When Estimating the Budgetary Effects of Legislation

The specific provisions of a new policy would greatly affect the number of people who received temporary-worker visas and, subsequently, the costs of a variety of federal services. Among the issues that CBO would consider when estimating the effects of such policy proposals are the following:

- Would family members of temporary workers be eligible for similar residency status?
- Would people be required to leave the country for some portion of the year?
- How much would it cost (in the form of fines or fees) to participate in the program?
- Would new types of visas or expanded numbers of visas for temporary workers be tied directly to those workers' employers?
- Would temporary workers ultimately be eligible for LPR status, citizenship, or some other long-term-resident status?
- What would the time frame be for achieving such status?
- What actions would temporary workers need to take to obtain status as an LPR?

Different combinations of policy changes could significantly affect the types of workers who entered the country. For example, a policy that required workers to pay a substantial fee and leave the United States for some period of time would be less onerous for those workers who have the means and capability to incur such costs and therefore are better equipped than other workers to adapt to such a policy.

Effects on Federal Spending and Revenues

Under current law, temporary workers are typically not eligible for many federal programs; thus, the direct impact on the federal budget of increasing the number of visas for temporary workers would probably be small in the short term. However, if legislation both expanded the number of available LPR visas and allowed temporary workers to adjust their status and eventually become citizens, the long-term fiscal impact of those residents and their citizen children could be significant. In addition to spending on program benefits, DHS would incur administrative costs to process visa applications, and SSA would incur costs to provide Social Security numbers and cards to temporary workers. The increased costs for DHS would be at least partially offset by collections from application fees. An increase in the number of temporary workers also might result in an increase in revenues from income and payroll taxes; however, temporary workers' tax liability would depend on the specific category of their visa and the length of time they have been in the country.

Health Care Programs for Low-Income People, SNAP, and SSI. Because of current program restrictions, temporary workers are not eligible for CHIP, SNAP, or SSI but are eligible for emergency Medicaid services if they meet other eligibility requirements for Medicaid. Because they are lawfully present in the United States, temporary workers may also be eligible to receive subsidies for health insurance through the insurance exchanges created by the ACA if they meet income requirements and do not have access to certain other sources of health insurance coverage. (However, if temporary workers are lawfully present in the country for a short time, they may be less likely to apply for and receive subsidies through the exchanges.) Hence, an increase in the number of visas for temporary workers would probably lead to higher federal spending for emergency Medicaid and subsidies for health insurance exchanges. In addition, depending on the economic situation of the household and other factors, children born in the United States to those new entrants might qualify for all five of the programs discussed here.

Social Security and Medicare

Depending on the proposed change to immigration policy, temporary workers might or might not be eligible for these programs. Changes that allowed temporary workers to qualify for such benefits would lead more of them to collect Social Security and Medicare benefits the longer they remained in the country—primarily because, as they aged, their likelihood of disability or retirement would rise. In the case of Social Security, such workers also would be more likely to have earned the necessary quarters of coverage to qualify for benefits. Under current law, most workers who gain LPR or citizenship status following admission as a temporary worker eventually qualify for Medicare.

Pell Grants and Federal Student Loans

Temporary workers are not eligible for federal student loans and grants. Thus, unless changes to the visa program were accompanied by changes in the eligibility requirements for those programs, changes to the number or type of temporary-worker visas would not result in more federal expenditures.

Unemployment Insurance

Temporary workers are generally eligible for unemployment insurance provided they remain legally eligible to work while they are unemployed. An increase in the number of temporary workers would result in a larger workforce. Therefore, the number of unemployed at a given unemployment rate would be greater and expenditures for unemployment insurance would be higher.

Refundable Tax Credits, Income Taxes, and Payroll Taxes

The tax liability of temporary workers in the United States depends on the specific category of their visa and how long they have been in the country. For example, foreign agricultural workers (holders of H-2A visas) are exempt from paying Social Security and Medicare taxes on income earned from agricultural work. Those workers may be responsible for federal income taxes depending on how long they have been in the country, the amount of income they earned in the United States, and other factors. Some temporary workers may be exempt from federal personal income taxes depending on their country of origin. Additionally, some temporary workers may be eligible for refundable tax credits, but that eligibility depends on a number of factors, including the type of work the person is authorized to undertake and the number of days he or she has spent in the United States.[43]

Granting Legal Status to Unauthorized Residents

The Congress has considered several policy options in the past that would confer some type of legal status on some of the roughly 11 million to 12 million noncitizens who live in the United States without authorization. Provisions of proposed legalization have typically included certain general eligibility requirements: For instance, people would have to prove that they have been in the country for a specified number of years or from a certain date, that they have successfully completed a security background check, that they have not been convicted of serious crimes while in the country, and that they have paid certain fines and fees.

In the past, CBO has estimated the budgetary effects of policies that would confer legal status on unauthorized residents in the following categories:

- People who are unlawfully present and working in the agricultural sector;
- People who entered the United States without authorization when they were young (for an example of such a proposal, see Box 3 on page 24); and
- Most other unauthorized residents, regardless of their occupation or age of entry.[44]

Factors CBO Considers When Estimating the Budgetary Effects of Legislation

The specific provisions of legalization policies, if implemented, would greatly affect the number of people who participate in federal programs as well as the costs of providing benefits and related government services. Among the issues CBO would consider when estimating the effects of such policy proposals are the following:

- Would the change in legal status be temporary or permanent?
- If previously unauthorized residents became LPRs, would they be eligible for the same benefits available to other LPRs or would the benefits be restricted?
- Would people granted legal status be eligible to become U.S. citizens?

- Would waiting periods for benefits be similar to those that exist under current law?
- Would spouses and children also be eligible for legal status? If so, would all dependents be eligible or only those who currently live in the country without authorization?
- How much would eligible people have to pay in fines or fees to participate in the program?

Effects on Federal Spending and Revenues

Whether, and to what extent, newly authorized residents qualified for federal benefits would have significant budgetary implications. Their eligibility for certain benefits would depend in part on whether they were granted temporary authorization or LPR status. Policies that provided currently unauthorized residents with LPR status or otherwise increased the number of residents with LPR status would result in more spending for federal programs. Legalization policies also might result in increased tax revenues, stemming mostly from some additional payment of income and payroll taxes.

Policies that allow currently unauthorized residents to become LPRs would, over time, increase spending for a variety of federal benefits, including those provided by health care programs for low-income people (specifically, Medicaid, CHIP, and subsidies for the purchase of health insurance through the exchanges established by the ACA), SNAP, Social Security, Medicare, and various refundable tax credits. Several other federal programs, such as SSI, Pell grants, and unemployment insurance also could experience spending increases. In accordance with current law, many of these programs already require applicants to demonstrate that they have lived in the country legally for a certain period. However, for the health insurance exchange subsidies, no such residency requirement applies to lawful residents. If the policy changing the status of currently unauthorized residents did not specifically make them ineligible for the subsidies, much of the budgetary impact in the first few years after enactment of a change in their status would stem from added costs for those subsidies. After that time, changes in spending for other programs would have increased importance.

In addition to increases in spending for benefits, government agencies would incur higher administrative and processing costs. For example, a policy that resulted in an increase in the number of visa applications would add to DHS's administrative costs, and providing newly authorized residents with

Social Security numbers and cards would lead to increases in costs for SSA. The additional costs incurred by DHS, however, might be offset by collections from application fees. Finally, proposals that required applicants to pay monetary penalties as well as application fees in order to change their legal status would result in additional revenues.

Health Care Programs for Low-Income People

Policies that conferred legal status on formerly unauthorized residents could result in increased spending for Medicaid, CHIP, and subsidies provided through the health insurance exchanges.

Unauthorized residents who are currently in the country already qualify for emergency Medicaid services if they meet income and other eligibility criteria. To the extent that legalization programs resulted in spouses and children entering the country, some of those new entrants also might qualify for emergency Medicaid services. If LPR status was a component of the legalization process, those LPRs who met income and other eligibility criteria would qualify for all medical services under Medicaid five years after becoming an LPR.

For children who are unauthorized, eligibility for CHIP depends on whether the state in which they live chooses to provide benefits to them. Therefore, policies that increased the number of lawfully present children in the United States could ultimately lead to higher enrollment in CHIP and could lead to greater federal spending for the program, assuming that sufficient funds were made available for the program. Many would have to wait five years to obtain full coverage.

Similarly, policies that increased the number of lawfully present people would result in more people qualifying for exchange subsidies; unless otherwise specified, they would be eligible for those subsidies without a waiting period. Because unauthorized workers tend to have lower incomes than other groups, many would probably have income low enough to qualify for generous exchange subsidies, if they lacked access to certain other sources of coverage (including Medicaid, CHIP, and affordable employment-based insurance) and met certain other requirements.

SNAP

If LPR status was a component of the legalization process, granting that status to children under the age of 18 would result in their immediately qualifying for SNAP benefits as long as they met the program's other eligibility requirements. If a policy was adopted that conferred LPR status on unauthorized residents over the age of 18 but maintained current eligibility rules— specifically, the five-year waiting period—those workers who met the program's other eligibility requirements could eventually receive SNAP benefits.

Social Security

People who are not lawfully present in the United States are barred from receiving Social Security benefits. Thus, under current law, those individuals may pay Social Security taxes but cannot qualify for retirement, disability, or survivors' benefits. If they are lawfully present, they can receive such benefits once they meet the program's requirements.

Box 3. Estimating the Effects of the DREAM Act on the Federal Budget

Previous estimates of proposed legislation that would change federal immigration policies related to young people illustrate how the Congressional Budget Office (CBO) projects the cost of such policies to the federal government. For example, in December 2010, CBO and the staff of the Joint Committee on Taxation (JCT) prepared cost estimates for two versions of the Development, Relief, and Education of Alien Minors Act of 2010 (DREAM Act).

Both bills (S. 3992 and H.R. 6497) would have provided conditional nonimmigrant status for unauthorized residents who met specific requirements:

- They were less than 16 years of age when they entered the country;
- They had lived in the United States for at least five years before the bill's enactment;
- They had graduated from high school, obtained a GED certificate, or were high school students who had been admitted to an institution of higher education; and
- They had completed background checks and paid any federal taxes due.

For the most part, the bills' eligibility requirements for conditional nonimmigrant status were similar, although the length of legal status and the fees charged for participation differed. The Senate bill would have provided conditional nonimmigrant status for 10 years. After 10 years, residents would be eligible for lawful permanent resident (LPR) status if they had received a college degree or served at least two years in the military.

The version of the legislation introduced in the House of Representatives would have provided conditional nonimmigrant status for an initial period of five years.

That status could have been extended for an additional five years if the individual had earned a degree, completed at least two years toward a bachelor's (or higher) degree, or served at least two years in the military. After the five-year extension, the resident would be eligible for LPR status.

When these proposals were being considered, CBO estimated that, by 2020, fewer residents would have been granted conditional nonimmigrant status under the provisions of the House bill (700,000 residents) than under the Senate proposal (1.1 million residents). Those differences reflect, among other factors, the likelihood that many people who would have obtained the initial five-year status in the House version would not have met the requirements for the extension.

The estimates of changes in federal revenues and spending depended on how many people CBO anticipated would attain conditional nonimmigrant status and subsequently become LPRs. By granting conditional nonimmigrant status to some previously unauthorized residents, both bills would have increased the number of authorized workers, thereby resulting in more revenues from individual and corporate income taxes and from social insurance taxes.

On balance, JCT estimated that the Senate bill would have increased federal revenues by $2.3 billion over 10 years, whereas the House bill, which affected fewer people, would have boosted revenues by $1.7 billion over 10 years.

Both bills would have also resulted in changes in direct spending for refundable tax credits, Social Security, Medicare, Pell grants, federal student loans, and activities of the Department of Homeland Security. CBO estimated that the Senate version would have increased net direct spending by about $1.1 billion over the 2011–2020 period, whereas the House version would have decreased net direct spending by about $500 million over the same period. (Direct spending is the budget authority provided by laws other than appropriation acts and the outlays that result from that budget authority.)

Thus, both bills would have resulted in changes in revenues and direct spending that would have reduced federal budget deficits in the 10 years following enactment. CBO estimated that, if implemented, both bills would have resulted in the eventual conversion of some conditional nonimmigrants to LPR status after 2020 and would have led to increased spending in subsequent years for subsidies provided through federal health insurance exchanges, Medicaid, and the Supplemental Nutrition Assistance Program.

Both bills would have specifically banned conditional nonimmigrants from participating in health insurance exchanges and receiving premium tax credits under the Affordable Care Act.1 Absent that specification, CBO would have estimated that both bills would have entailed significant spending by the federal government for those subsidies.

Future estimates for similar legislation would probably differ because of recent administrative changes implemented by the Department of Homeland Security (see Box 1 on page 9).

[1] As referred to in this report, the Affordable Care Act comprises the Patient Protection and Affordable Care Act (Public Law 111-148) and the health care provisions of the Health Care and Education Reconciliation Act of 2010 (P.L. 111-152), as affected by subsequent judicial decisions, statutory changes, and administrative actions.

Proposals that would grant lawful presence to many unauthorized workers could increase the number of future Social Security beneficiaries. Various sources— data from the Census Bureau's Current Population Survey, research by the Pew Hispanic Center, and studies involving people who obtained legal status under the Immigration Reform and Control Act of 1986—indicate that those workers tend to be younger than the rest of the S. workforce.[45] Because younger workers are less likely to qualify for and claim Social Security benefits than older workers, CBO expects that relatively few of the people directly affected by legalization proposals would qualify for Social Security retirement, disability, or survivors' benefits in the near term, although those numbers would grow in subsequent years. Some proposals could prohibit any unauthorized employment undertaken by such individuals from counting toward their eligibility for Social Security even if they did eventually receive authorization to work. The ability or inability of a formerly unauthorized worker to apply those employment periods to future benefits would affect federal outlays for the program. In addition, depending on the specific provisions of the legislation, people who previously paid Social Security taxes using a stolen or fake Social Security number might be able to claim benefits in the future by using a legitimate Social Security number or by claiming credits earned while using a fraudulent Social Security number.

SSI

Because adults' eligibility for SSI requires five years of lawful permanent residency and a work history spanning 10 years for those who have not naturalized, conferring legal status on currently unauthorized residents would initially affect the SSI program mostly by increasing the rate at which their U.S.–born children received program benefits. (Their foreign-born children also must spend five years as LPRs to receive benefits. Foreign-born children who do not meet that residency requirement would not be eligible for benefits unless their eligibility was specified in the legislation.) Although the U.S.–born children are already citizens by virtue of their birth in the United States, their parents might be more willing to seek benefits for their offspring once they themselves attained legal status.

Medicare

As with Social Security, proposals that would grant lawful presence to unauthorized residents would result in a small increase in the number of Medicare beneficiaries in the near term but have a greater impact in the longer term as those workers aged and then claimed benefits. In addition, depending on the exact nature of the policy change, people who qualified for Social Security Disability Insurance also might be eligible for Medicare after a two-year waiting period.46 Some people, however, might choose to move back to the country in which they were born (or to some other country outside of the United States) and would therefore no longer qualify for benefits.

Pell Grants and Federal Student Loans

LPRs are eligible to receive federal student aid on the same basis as citizens. Hence, allowing the number of LPRs in the country to grow would probably boost the number of people who apply for such aid. Legalization policies that increased the number of LPRs or conditional permanent residents could boost enrollment at postsecondary institutions as newly eligible students qualified for federal grants and loans.

Unemployment Insurance

Unauthorized workers are not eligible to receive unemployment insurance benefits if they lose a job. An increase in the number of authorized workers would affect outlays for unemployment insurance benefits by increasing the number of people who could be eligible for benefits in the future, assuming they met other eligibility criteria as determined by their state. Because states finance the cost of most unemployment benefits through taxes on employment (both of which are reflected in the federal budget), the net effect on the federal budget from any increase in unemployment benefits that stemmed from changes in immigration would be small.

Refundable Tax Credits

Granting lawful presence and work authorization to unauthorized residents would probably increase the total amount of refundable tax credits provided through the tax system. Relative to native-born citizens and foreign-born residents authorized to be in the United States, a higher proportion of unauthorized workers would be eligible for refundable tax credits because they tend to have lower income than other groups. In addition, once granted legal status, more formerly unauthorized workers would probably earn taxable income instead of receiving informal payments that are not reported to the IRS; that change might make them eligible for such tax credits.

Income and Payroll Taxes

According to one estimate, at least half of unauthorized residents pay income taxes and Social Security taxes through their employer (even though they are not eligible to receive Social Security benefits).[47] If some were granted legal status, the proportion paying income and payroll taxes would probably increase. In addition, more revenues would probably be generated if the policy allowed spouses and children of unauthorized immigrants who were not currently in the United States to enter the country and work.

Proposals Related to Enforcement and Workplace Verification

Proposals to address the enforcement of immigration law generally aim to enhance border security and internal enforcement, and to improve systems and procedures for verifying employees' legal status at the workplace. The budgetary effects of such proposals would depend on the costs of implementing them and on their effectiveness in reducing the number of unauthorized residents; a reduction in the number of unauthorized residents would decrease costs for certain federal programs but also would result in a loss of federal tax receipts. Funding for such proposals could be provided in immigration legislation (which would result in outlays categorized as mandatory spending) or could depend on annual appropriation acts (which would result in outlays categorized as discretionary spending).

Increasing Border Security and Internal Enforcement

Slowing the flow of illegal immigration into the United States and decreasing the employment of unauthorized residents would require the development and implementation of well-designed and well-coordinated programs and processes. The goal of such programs and procedures would be twofold: to make it more difficult for people to enter the country without authorization; and to make it easier for officials to identify, locate, and remove those who entered without authorization or who remained after their authorized stay had ended. Funding for border security has risen sharply in recent years, and estimated net flows of unauthorized migrants to the United States have fallen in recent years. However, it is unclear how much of that decrease is attributable to stepped-up enforcement activities and how much is attributable to the downturn in employment associated with the global recession, or to other factors.[48]

Policies That Would Increase Border Security and Internal Enforcement

Policies designed to enhance border security and internal enforcement generally focus on the following four activities: increasing the number of personnel responsible for enforcement, improving border infrastructure and technologies, expanding identification systems, and improving cooperation with state and local governments.

More Personnel

Employing and training additional people to enforce U.S. immigration laws and prosecute violators would require increased federal spending for those purposes. For example, CBO has analyzed several proposals that would have included funding for additional Border Patrol agents (to increase the interdiction of people trying to enter the country illegally) and additional federal judges (to speed up the process of removing people in violation of immigration laws).[49]

Improved Border Infrastructure and Technologies

Improving the kinds and amount of equipment, infrastructure, and technology that are used to secure the country's borders also would necessitate increased federal spending. Such improvements could include, for example, building and maintaining border fences, deploying additional mobile, video, and other surveillance systems, and deploying and operating manned and unmanned aerial vehicles.

Expanded Identification Systems

The Pew Hispanic Center has estimated that 40 percent to 50 percent of people who are now residing in the United States without authorization entered the country by legal means.50 Therefore, a more effective immigration control program could involve additional internal enforcement aimed at identifying those people, as well as improved border security (see Box 4).

Improved Cooperation with State and Local Governments

To implement immigration-related enforcement activities, the federal government sometimes provides training to state and local law enforcement officers.[51] For example, the Section 287(g) program authorizes the federal government to enter into agreements with state and local law enforcement agencies.[52] Those agreements allow police officers to screen individuals who have been charged with nonimmigration offenses to determine if they are in violation of immigration law. Authorized officers are able to search selected federal databases and conduct interviews to assist in the identification of people living in the country illegally. In 2012, DHS announced that it would not renew the 287(g) task force agreements because other programs, such as Secure Communities, were more effective.

Factors CBO Considers When Estimating the Budgetary Effects of Legislation

When assessing the impact of proposed changes to border and internal enforcement policies, CBO would consider the following:

- To what extent would the policy require new enforcement activities at different points of entry?
- Would the policy require that additional federal employees be hired and, if so, at what cost?
- Given the complexities involved in hiring and training immigration law enforcement officials, including high rates of turnover, is it feasible to sustain new, higher staffing levels?

- Would the policy require the creation of new technology for border surveillance?
- Does the policy include provisions to identify people who remain in the country after their authorization to do so has expired?
- To what degree would the policy require the federal government to compensate state and local governments for enforcing immigration law?
- How effective would the policy be at diminishing the net inflow of unauthorized residents?

Effects on Federal Spending and Revenues

Implementing such policies would require increased funding, the amount of which would depend on the number of additional federal employees that would be needed and the costs to develop and acquire whatever facilities and equipment would be necessary. In addition, increased border security and other enforcement measures—as well as a mandatory employment verification system to deter the hiring of unauthorized workers (discussed in the next section)—could affect the federal budget by changing the net flow of unauthorized residents into the country. On the one hand, fewer people might enter illegally because crossing the border would be more difficult and remaining in the country would be harder without legal status. On the other hand, tighter border enforcement might encourage people to stay in the United States because it would be harder to get back in. And the enactment of legislation that included provisions conferring legal status on those in the country unlawfully might encourage more people to try to enter the United States illegally (in the hope of benefiting from a future legalization program).

The resulting budgetary effects are difficult to assess. They would depend on a number of factors about which there is little reliable information: the number of illegal border crossings that would occur under current law; the extent to which new enforcement activities would defer, delay, or otherwise modify the behavior of potential unlawful border-crossers; and how administrative and enforcement procedures would change in response to those behaviors.

In the past, CBO has estimated that wide-ranging changes in immigration policy would reduce the net annual flow of unauthorized residents by one-quarter.[53] More recently, CBO estimated that the Border Security, Economic Opportunity, and Immigration Modernization Act, as passed by the Senate in

2013, would reduce the net annual flow of unauthorized residents by between one-third and one-half.[54] The estimated impact of any future legislation on those flows will depend on CBO's judgment of what the net flows of unauthorized migrants would be under current law and an assessment of how the proposed legislation would affect those flows. CBO's earlier estimates of those effects may or may not be applicable to future proposals. Estimated net flows of unauthorized migrants to the United States have fallen to nearly zero or even reversed in recent years—that is, more unauthorized residents may have left the country than have arrived.[55] Those developments are attributable to a variety of factors, including the downturn in employment associated with the global recession and changes in U.S. border security.

Decreases in the net inflows of unauthorized migrants would lead to reduced spending on emergency Medicaid services and child nutrition programs because fewer people would receive benefits. But some unauthorized residents pay payroll and income taxes, so a reduction in their number also might result in a loss of tax revenues.

Improving Verification of People's Eligibility to Work

Some proposals to reduce the number of unauthorized residents in the United States focus on making unlawful presence less attractive by restricting access to employment and increasing the security of identity documents. Under current law, noncitizens must have explicit employment authorization to work in the United States, and employers are not allowed to hire unauthorized workers. However, an estimated 8 million unauthorized residents work in the country.[56] Some employers knowingly hire unauthorized workers whereas others cannot detect fraudulent or fraudulently used documentation.

Under current law, newly hired workers must present two forms of identification to their employers and complete an I-9 form attesting that they are eligible to work in the United States. About two dozen documents can be accepted as proof of identity; but the issuing agent is not required to verify the legitimacy of those documents. Unauthorized workers can procure fraudulent documents or use authentic documents that were falsely obtained to satisfy the I-9 requirements.

The E-Verify program, administered by DHS, is an online system that employers can use to confirm that newly hired employees are eligible to work. Participation in the system is voluntary for most employers. Federal agencies and contractors, as well as some companies that have been found in violation of hiring laws, are required to use E-verify. In addition, some state and local governments have required employers in their jurisdiction to use the system.[57] As of January 2015, almost 570,000 employers were registered users of the E-Verify program, representing more than 1.8 million hiring sites. In fiscal year 2014, the E-Verify system processed more than 28 million queries.[58]

Factors CBO Considers When Estimating the Budgetary Effects of Proposed Legislation

When estimating the cost of proposals to change work verification systems, CBO would consider the following questions:

- Would the new system be mandatory for all employees or would it apply only to those who are newly hired?
- How many people would need to have their status verified?
- Does the existing E-Verify system have the capacity to confirm the status of all employees or would changes be necessary?
- Would a new system rely on existing identification documents, or would federal agencies be required to supply new ones?
- Would biometric identifiers—which identify people by their physical characteristics or traits, such as fingerprints, handprints, or DNA—be required?
- What recourse or compensation would be available to workers who were incorrectly identified as not authorized to work?

Effects on Federal Spending and Revenues

If all employers were required to use the E-Verify system, and if employers needed to confirm the status of all employees, DHS would need additional resources for staff, technological components, and overhead to handle the increased workload. The Social Security Administration also would need additional resources to upgrade technology and hire new employees to resolve issues that arose when E-verify could not confirm that a person was eligible for work.

Expanding the E-Verify system without other changes to current policy would probably result in decreased federal revenues because it would probably lead to an increase in the number of unauthorized workers being paid outside of the tax system. Some employers who currently withhold income and payroll taxes from the wages of unauthorized workers and report those amounts to the IRS through the use of an ITIN or other employee identification number would no longer withhold or report such taxes.

Appendix: Recent Congressional Budget Office Reports on Immigration and Selected Cost Estimates for Legislation Related to Immigration

Reports

The Economic Impact of S. 744, the Border Security, Economic Opportunity, and Immigration Modernization Act (June 2013), www.cbo.gov/publication/44346.

A Description of the Immigrant Population—2013 Update (attachment to a letter to the Honorable Paul Ryan, May 8, 2013), www.cbo.gov/publication/44134.

Letter to the Honorable Paul Ryan describing how CBO would analyze the economic effects of proposals to make major changes in immigration policy (May 2, 2013), www.cbo.gov/publication/44109.

A Description of the Immigrant Population: An Update (June 2011), www.cbo.gov/publication/41453.

Migrants' Remittances and Related Economic Flows (February 2011), www.cbo.gov/publication/22012.

Immigration Policy in the United States: An Update (December 2010), www.cbo.gov/publication/21921.

The Role of Immigrants in the U.S. Labor Market: An Update (July 2010), www.cbo.gov/publication/21656.

Cost Estimates

Cost estimate for H.R. 5759, the Preventing Executive Overreach on Immigration Act of 2014 (December 3, 2014), www.cbo.gov/ publication/49822.

Cost estimate for H.R. 15, the Border Security, Economic Opportunity, and Immigration Modernization Act (March 25, 2014), www.cbo.gov/ publication/45206.

Cost estimate for H.R. 2131, the Supplying Knowledge-Based Immigrants and Lifting Levels of STEM Visas Act (SKILLS Visa Act) (March 12, 2014), www.cbo.gov/ publication/45179.

Cost estimate for H.R. 2278, the Strengthen and Fortify Enforcement Act (December 5, 2013), www.cbo.gov/ publication/44942.

Cost estimate for H.R. 1772, the Legal Workforce Act (December 17, 2013), www.cbo.gov/publication/44980.

Letter to the Honorable Patrick J. Leahy providing an estimate for S. 744, the Border Security, Economic Opportunity, and Immigration Modernization Act, as passed by the Senate on June 27, 2013 (July 3, 2013), www.cbo.gov/publication/44397.

Cost estimate for Senate Amendment 1183 to S. 744, the Border Security, Economic Opportunity, and Immigration Modernization Act (June 24, 2013), http://www.cbo.gov/publication/44372.

Cost estimate for S. 744, the Border Security, Economic Opportunity, and Immigration Modernization Act (June 18, 2013), www.cbo.gov/ publication/44225.

Cost estimate for H.R. 6429, the STEM Jobs Act of 2012 (November 28, 2012), www.cbo.gov/publication/ 43740.

Cost estimate for H.R. 6497, the Development, Relief, and Education for Alien Minors Act of 2010 (December 8, 2010), www.cbo.gov/publication/ 21976.

Cost estimate for S. 3992, the Development, Relief, and Education for Alien Minors Act of 2010 (December 7, 2010), www.cbo.gov/publication/ 21973.

Cost estimate for Senate Amendment 1150 to S. 1348, the Comprehensive Immigration Reform Act of 2007 (June 4, 2007), www.cbo.gov/ publication/18716.

Cost estimate for S. 2611, the Comprehensive Immigration Reform Act of 2006 (August 18, 2006), www.cbo.gov/publication/18065.

GLOSSARY

Conditional permanent resident: A noncitizen who gains entrance to the United States because he or she has married a U.S. citizen or a lawful permanent resident, or has invested in a U.S. business. Status as a conditional permanent resident conveys the right to live and work in the United States for two years on a probationary basis. Conditional permanent residents have the same rights and responsibilities as permanent residents, but they must apply to remove the conditions placed on their permanent residence status after two years.

Deferred action: A process by which the Department of Homeland Security delays removal proceedings for unauthorized residents. Those who are approved for deferred action are considered lawfully present in the country but do not gain legal status.

Foreign born: Born outside the United States (or one of its territories) to parents who are not U.S. citizens.

Green card: A wallet-sized card showing that the bearer is a lawful permanent resident of the United States.

Lawful permanent resident (LPR): A noncitizen of the United States who is authorized to live, work, and study in the United States permanently. Such status is granted to immediate relatives of U.S. citizens (including spouses, minor children, and parents). It can also be granted on the basis of the following: family-sponsored preferences (for example, to extended family members, such as aunts or cousins); employment-based preferences; and diversity preferences.

The number of people who can be granted LPR status based on family-sponsored preferences, employment-based preferences, or diversity is subject to annual limits; by contrast, the number of people who can be granted LPR status each year because they are immediate relatives of U.S. citizens or for humanitarian reasons is unlimited. After becoming an LPR, a noncitizen immigrant receives a permanent resident card, commonly called a green card, which serves as proof of permission to live and work in the country.

Lawfully present: Foreign-born noncitizens who have met the requisite criteria for admission to the United States and, once admitted, have not stayed beyond the period originally authorized; or those who have current permission from the Citizenship and Immigration Services to stay or live in the United States.

Migrant: A person who moves to a country other than that of his or her usual residence, whether legally or illegally.

Native born: Born in the United States or one of its territories or, if born abroad, the child of at least one parent who is a U.S. citizen.

Naturalized citizen: A foreign-born person who has become a U.S. citizen by fulfilling requirements set forth in the Immigration and Nationality Act, including, in most cases, having resided in the United States for at least five years.

Noncitizen: Encompasses two categories of foreign-born people—those who are authorized to live and work in the United States either temporarily or permanently (see "conditional permanent resident," "lawful permanent resident," "temporary resident or visitor," "temporary worker," and "refugee or asylum-seeker"); and those who are not authorized to live or work in the United States (see "unauthorized resident").

Qualified alien: As defined in the Personal Responsibility and Work Opportunity Reconciliation Act of 1996, a subset of noncitizens that are eligible for public benefit programs, such as the Supplemental Nutrition Assistance Program and Medicaid. Qualified aliens primarily include LPRs, refugees, and people who have been granted asylum. Most other categories of noncitizens— including temporary residents and visitors as well as all unauthorized residents—are not considered qualified aliens.

Refugee or asylum-seeker: A person who has been persecuted in his or her home country or who has a well-founded fear of persecution in that country on the basis of race, religion, nationality, membership in a particular social group, or political opinion. Such individuals who are outside of the United States apply for refugee status. Those who are inside of the United States apply for asylum.

Removal: The expulsion of a foreign-born individual from the United States if he or she is found to be inadmissible at a port of entry or otherwise in violation of U.S. immigration laws. An inadmissible individual is a person who seeks entry but does not meet the criteria of the Immigration and Nationality Act.

Temporary resident or visitor: A noncitizen who is admitted to the United States with a temporary visa or who is allowed to enter the country without a visa. People in those categories include visitors who are in the United States for short periods and temporary residents who are in the United States for longer, although still time-limited, stays.

Temporary worker: A noncitizen who is admitted to the United States with a temporary visa for purposes of time-limited employment.

Unauthorized resident: A noncitizen of the United States who is in the country without legal authorization. This category includes people who enter the country illegally and those who enter with valid visas but overstay their authorized time in the country. In this report, the category also encompasses those formerly unauthorized residents who have been approved for deferred action; they are lawfully present without legal status for the duration of their deferral.

U.S. visa: A permit allowing the bearer to apply for entry to the United States under a certain classification. Examples of those visa classifications include: student (F), visitor (B), and temporary worker (H).The Department of State is responsible for issuing visas at U.S. embassies and consulates outside of the United States. A visa does not grant the bearer the right to enter the United States. Officials with the Department of Homeland Security's Customs and Border Protection determine whether an individual can be admitted to the United States at a port of entry. A person may be denied entry by an official because he or she lacks proper documentation, because of public health or security concerns, or for other reasons.

End Notes

[1] See the glossary on page 35 for details about key terms used in this report.

[2] As referred to in this report, the ACA comprises the Patient Protection and Affordable Care Act (Public Law 111-148) and the health care provisions of the Health Care and Education Reconciliation Act of 2010 (P.L. 111-152), as affected by subsequent judicial decisions, statutory changes, and administrative actions.

[3] See section 2(c) of H. Res. 5, adopted on January 6, 2015, which added clause 8 to Rule XIII. The rule defines major legislation to include bills that would have a gross budgetary effect (before incorporating macroeconomic effects) in a fiscal year equal to or greater than 0.25 percent of GDP—or legislation so designated by certain committee chairmen. However, the rule does not apply to appropriation bills.

[4] For more details on these different types of noncitizens, see Congressional Budget Office, A Description of the Immigrant Population—2013 Update (May 2013), www.cbo.gov/ publication/ 44134, and Immigration Policy in the United States: An Update (December 2010), www.cbo.gov/publication/21921. In this report, unauthorized residents include those who have been approved for deferred action; they are lawfully present without legal status for the duration of their deferral.

[5] Estimates of the number of people granted LPR status on an annual basis are from Randall Monger and James Yankay, U.S. Lawful Permanent Residents: 2013 (Department of Homeland Security, Office of Immigration Statistics, May 2014), http://go.usa.gov/eDeA (PDF, 267 KB). For a discussion of undercounts of the noncitizen population in the ACA data set, see Michael Hoefer, Nancy Rytina, and Bryan Baker, Estimates of the

Unauthorized Immigrant Population Residing in the United States: January 2011 (Department of Homeland Security, Office of Immigration Statistics, March 2012), http://go.usa.gov/Zs9J. The number of LPRs, legal temporary workers, and unauthorized residents may not sum to the total noncitizen population because of differences in data sets. (For example, for this report, CBO obtained data on LPRs and unauthorized populations from DHS and data on the noncitizen population from the Census Bureau's American Community Survey.) Other differences are attributable to variations in methodology and probable undercounts of the noncitizen population.

[6] Many comprehensive immigration reform bills in recent years have focused on the broader categories of lawful immigration or unauthorized residents but have not typically called for changes in humanitarian immigration; however, S. 744 included provisions that would change the rules applying to that category. Changes to humanitarian immigration are often addressed in other bills.

[7] Based on data from Department of State, Bureau of Consular Affairs, Report of the Visa Office 2013, Table XVI(B), http://go.usa.gov/eDJC (PDF, 147 KB).

[8] DHS arrived at its estimate by calculating the difference between the total foreign-born population and the authorized foreign-born population. For those estimates, see Bryan Baker and Nancy Rytina, Estimates of the Unauthorized Immigrant Population Residing in the United States: January 2012 (Department of Homeland Security, Office of Immigration Statistics, March 2013), http://go.usa.gov/eDS3 (PDF, 194 KB). The numbers that form the basis of DHS's estimate, however, came from a variety of sources, and they involved various assumptions. Moreover, because they do not reflect actual population counts, the resulting estimates are subject to considerable uncertainty. The Pew Hispanic Center also estimates the number of unauthorized workers in the United States; its most recent estimate for 2012 is about 200,000 lower than the estimate by DHS. See Jeffrey S. Passel, D'Vera Cohn, and Molly Rohal, Unauthorized Immigrant Totals Rise in 7 States, Fall in 14 (Pew Hispanic Center, November 18, 2014), http://tinyurl.com/nf9mwzf (PDF, 2.33 MB).

[9] Pew Hispanic Center, Modes of Entry for the Unauthorized Population (May 2006), http://tinyurl.com/korn9w9.

[10] Demographic information presented here is based on data from the Census Bureau's 2013 American Community Survey as extracted from the Minnesota Population Center's Integrated Public Use Microdata Series. Unemployment information is based on data from outgoing rotation groups of the Census Bureau's monthly Current Population Survey, January 1994 to December 2013.

[11]. Estimates of the unauthorized population are from Bryan Baker and Nancy Rytina, Estimates of the Unauthorized Immigrant Population Residing in the United States: January 2012 (Department of Homeland Security, Office of Immigration Statistics, March 2013), http://go.usa.gov/eDS3 (PDF, 673 KB).

[12]. See Congressional Budget Office, A Description of the Immigrant Population—2013 Update (attachment to a letter to the Honorable Paul Ryan, May 8, 2013), www.cbo.gov/publication/ 44134, A Description of the Immigrant Population: An Update (June 2011), Exhibit 14, www.cbo.gov/publication/41453, and The Role of Immigrants in the U.S. Labor Market: An Update (July 2010), www.cbo.gov/publication/21656.

[13]. Limits on noncitizens' eligibility to receive some federal benefits were established in title IY of the Personal Responsibility and Work Opportunity Reconciliation Act of 1996, P.L. 104-193, 110 Stat. 2260.

[14]. See Leighton Ku and Brian Bruen, Poor Immigrants Use Public Benefits at a Lower Rate Than Poor Native-Born Citizens, Economic Development Bulletin 17 (Cato Institute, Center for Global Liberty and Prosperity, March 4, 2013), http:// tinyurl.com/bfpbsmn.

[15] See, for example, Randolph Capps and others, The Health and Well-Being of Young Children of Immigrants (Urban Institute, February 8, 2005), www.urban.org/publications/ 311139.html; and Michael E. Fix and Jeffrey S. Passel, Trends in Noncitizens' and Citizens' Use of Public Benefits Following Welfare Reform, 1994–97 (Urban Institute, March 1999), www.urban.org/publications/ 408086.html.

[16] See Congressional Budget Office, The 2014 Long-Term Budget Outlook (July 2014), pp. 29–31, www.cbo.gov/publication/ 45471.

[17] The ACA gives states the option to expand eligibility for Medicaid to nonelderly residents with income up to 133 percent of the federal poverty level, commonly referred to as the FPL, which currently is $23,850 for a family of four. The act defines the income used to determine eligibility in a way that effectively increases that threshold to 138 percent of the FPL.

[18] See, for example, Karina Fortuny and Ajay Chaudry, A Comprehensive Review of Immigrant Access to Health and Human Services (Urban Institute, June 2011), www.urban.org/ publications/412425.html.

[19] See 26 U.S.C. §36B (c)(1)(B) (2012).

[20] See Congressional Budget Office, The Supplemental Nutrition Assistance Program (April 2012), www.cbo.gov/publication/43173. Additionally, eligible children can receive nutrition assistance through various child nutrition programs—including the National School Lunch Program and the School Breakfast Program, among others—regardless of their legal status. Thus, any change in the total number of children in the country would affect spending for those programs.

[21] See Congressional Budget Office, The 2014 Long-Term Budget Outlook (July 2014), Chapter 3, www.cbo.gov/publication/45471, and Social Security Disability Insurance: Participation Trends and Their Fiscal Implications (July 2010), www.cbo.gov/publication/ 21638.

[22] Section 402 of the Personal Responsibility and Work Opportunity Reconciliation Act of 1996, P.L. 104-193, 8 U.S.C. § 1611(a) (2012).

[23] See Social Security Administration, Social Security: Your Payments While You Are Outside the United States (September 2013), http://go.usa.gov/BaXJ.

[24] See Congressional Budget Office, Supplemental Security Income: An Overview (December 2012), www.cbo.gov/publication/43759.

[25] See Department of Education, "Completing the Free Application for Federal Student Aid (FAFSA), 2013–14" (updated February 5, 2013), http://go.usa.gov/Bx2W.

[26] See Congressional Budget Office, The Pell Grant Program: Recent Growth and Policy Options (September 2013), www.cbo.gov/ publication/44448, and Costs and Policy Options for Federal Student Loan Programs (March 2010), www.cbo.gov/publication/ 21018.

[27] See Congressional Budget Office, Unemployment Insurance in the Wake of the Recent Recession (November 2012), www.cbo.gov/ publication/43734.

[28] In contrast with temporary workers, temporary residents whose authorization to be in the United States depends on employment are not necessarily eligible for unemployment compensation.

[29] National Employment Law Project, "Immigrants' Eligibility for Unemployment Compensation" (April 2002), http://tinyurl.com/ d6otr2a.

[30] For more information about refundable tax credits, see Congressional Budget Office, Refundable Tax Credits (January 2013), www.cbo.gov/publication/43767.

[31] Taxpayers cannot claim the EITC if the following conditions exist: their Social Security card states "Not Valid for Employment" and their Social Security number was issued specifically so that the taxpayer (and his or her spouse and qualifying children) could get a federally funded benefit, such as Medicaid. See Internal Revenue Service, "Earned Income Credit (EIC)," Publication 596 (December 2014), http://go.usa.gov/Ba5e.

[32] The IRS issues ITINs to people who are required to have such identification for tax purposes but are not eligible to obtain a Social Security number because they are not authorized to work. According to a recent report by the Congressional Research Service, it is unclear how many individuals who file taxes with ITINs were unauthorized residents or part of mixed-status families that include both citizens and unauthorized residents. See Congressional Research Service, Ability of Unauthorized Aliens to Claim Refundable Tax Credits (July 2012). In January 2013, the IRS tightened the documentation requirements for obtaining an ITIN.

[33] According to a study of the effects on the wages of workers who gained legal status as a result of the 1986 Immigration Reform and Control Act, "The postlegalization changes in wage determinants for legalized workers are consistent with labor market mobility, which provides workers with an opportunity to move into jobs that reward existing human capital." See Sherrie A. Kossoudji and Deborah A. Cobb-Clark, "Coming Out of the Shadows: Learning About Legal Status and Wages From the Legalized Population," Journal of Labor Economics, vol. 20, no. 3 (July 2002), p. 618, http://tinyurl.com/kaqesty; and Congressional Budget Office, The Economic Impact of S. 744, the Border Security, Economic Opportunity, and Immigration Modernization Act (June 2013), www.cbo.gov/publication/44346.

[34] See Economic Report of the President, 2005 (February 2005), Chapter 4, p. 107, http://tinyurl.com/c9kdark; Social Security Administration, Office of the Chief Actuary, "Letter to Senator Richard J. Durbin" (June 5, 2007). Also see Alice H. Wade and others, "Projections of Immigration for the 2008 Social Security Trustees Report," Actuarial Note 148 (Social Security Administration, Office of the Chief Actuary, March 2009), http://go.usa.gov/BaRG.

[35] See Congressional Budget Office, letter to the Honorable Patrick J. Leahy providing an estimate for S. 744, the Border Security, Economic Opportunity, and Immigration Modernization Act, as passed by the Senate on June 27, 2013 (July 3, 2013), www.cbo.gov/publication/44397; cost estimate for S. 744, the Border Security, Economic Opportunity, and Immigration Modernization Act (June 18, 2013), http://www.cbo.gov/publication/44225; and letter to the Honorable Paul Ryan describing how CBO would analyze the economic effects of proposals to make major changes in economic policy (May 2, 2013), www.cbo.gov/publication/44109. In addition, see Congressional Budget Office, cost estimate for S. 2611, the Comprehensive Immigration Reform Act of 2006, and Additional Information on the Estimated Budgetary and Economic Effects of S. 2611 (attachments to a letter to the Honorable Charles E. Grassley, May 16, 2006), www.cbo.gov/publication/17779.

[36] See, for example, Congressional Budget Office, The Economic Impact of S. 744, the Border Security, Economic Opportunity, and Immigration Modernization Act (June 2013), www.cbo.gov/ publication/44346, and Additional Information on the Estimated Budgetary and Economic Effects of S. 2611 (attachment to a letter to the Honorable Charles E. Grassley, May 16, 2006), www.cbo.gov/publication/17779.

[37] See section 2(c) of H. Res. 5, adopted on January 6, 2015, which added clause 8 to Rule XIII. 37 The rule defines major legislation to include bills that would have a gross budgetary

effect (before incorporating macroeconomic effects) in a fiscal year equal to or greater than 0.25 percent of GDP—or legislation so designated by certain committee chairmen. However, the rule does not apply to appropriation bills.

[38] There are separate wait times for certain countries such as China, India, Mexico, and the Philippines. See http://travel.state.gov/ visa/bulletin/bulletin_1360.html.

[39] S. 744, 113th Congress (2013). That point system included various criteria such as employment history, education, the ability to speak English, knowledge of civics, and extended family considerations. Until the available visas were exhausted, visas would be awarded to those applicants with the highest scores. Changes in the skill mix of new LPRs could have other effects on the labor force, including raising productivity among other workers; see Congressional Budget Office, The Economic Impact of S. 744, the Border Security, Economic Opportunity, and Immigration Modernization Act (June 2013), www.cbo.gov/publication/44346.

[40] For an example of a proposal for such a commission, see Demetrios G. Papademetriou and others, "Harnessing the Advantages of Immigration for a 21st-Century Economy: A Standing Commission on Labor Markets, Economic Competitiveness, and Immigration" (Immigration Policy Institute, May 2009), http://tinyurl.com/2e7q2vw.

[41] Based on data from the Department of State, Bureau of Consular Affairs, Report of the Visa Office 2013, Table XVI(B), http://go.usa.gov/eDJC (PDF, 147 KB).

[42] In fiscal year 2012, nearly all H-1B visa holders had at least a bachelor's degree, and their median earnings were $70,000. See Department of Homeland Security, Characteristics of H-1B Specialty Occupation Workers (June 2013), http://go.usa.gov/eWaw (PDF, 500 KB). By comparison, CBO reported that in calendar year 2011 median earnings were $31,000 among foreign-born men and $24,000 among foreign-born women; see Congressional Budget Office, A Description of the Immigrant Population—2013 Update (attachment to a letter to the Honorable Paul Ryan, May 8, 2013), www.cbo.gov/publication/44134.

[43] See Internal Revenue Service, "U.S. Tax Guide for Aliens," Publication 519 (last updated January 13, 2015), www.irs.gov/ pub519.

[44] See, for example, Congressional Budget Office, letter to the Honorable Patrick J. Leahy providing an estimate for S. 744, the Border Security, Economic Opportunity, and Immigration Modernization Act, as passed by the Senate on June 27, 2013 (July 3, 2013), www.cbo.gov/publication/44397; cost estimate for S. 744, the Border Security, Economic Opportunity, and Immigration Modernization Act (June 18, 2013), www.cbo.gov/ publication/44225; cost estimate for S. 3992, the Development, Relief, and Education for Alien Minors Act of 2010 (December 2010), www.cbo.gov/publication/21952; cost estimate for Senate Amendment 1150 to S. 1348, the Comprehensive Immigration Reform Act of 2007 (June 4, 2007), www.cbo.gov/publication/ 18716; and cost estimate for S. 2611, the Comprehensive Immigration Reform Act of 2006 (August 2006), www.cbo.gov/ publication/18065.

[45] See, for example, Sherrie A. Kossoudji and Deborah A. Cobb-Clark, "Coming Out of the Shadows: Learning About Legal Status and Wages From the Legalized Population," Journal of Labor Economics, vol. 20, no. 3 (2002), http://tinyurl.com/ kaqesty; and Nancy Rytina, "IRCA Legalization Effects: Lawful Permanent Residence and Naturalization Through 2001" (paper presented at a conference on the Effects of Immigrant Legalization Programs on the United States: Scientific Evidence on Immigrant Adaptation and Impacts on U.S. Economy and Society, National Institutes of Health, October 25, 2002), http://tinyurl.com/ ls4vtvx.

[46] See Congressional Budget Office, Policy Options for the Social Security Disability Insurance Program (July 2012), www.cbo.gov/ publication/43421, and Social Security Disability Insurance: Participation Trends and Their Fiscal Implications (July 2010), www.cbo.gov/ publication/21638.

[47] See Economic Report of the President, 2005 (February 2005), http://tinyurl.com/c9kdark.

[48] See, for example, Jeffrey S. Passel, D'Vera Cohn, and Ana Gonzalez-Barrera, Net Migration From Mexico Falls to Zero— And Perhaps Less (Pew Hispanic Center, April 23, 2012), http://tinyurl.com/cfcka2j.

[49] See, for example, Congressional Budget Office, letter to the Honorable Patrick J. Leahy providing an estimate for S. 744, the Border Security, Economic Opportunity, and Immigration Modernization Act, as passed by the Senate on June 27, 2013 (July 3, 2013), www.cbo.gov/publication/44397; cost estimate for Senate amendment 1150 to S. 1348, the Comprehensive Immigration Reform Act of 2007 (June 4, 2007), www.cbo.gov/ publication/18716; cost estimate for S. 2611, the Comprehensive Immigration Reform Act of 2006 (August 18, 2006), www.cbo.gov/publication/18065; cost estimate for H.R. 4437, the Border Protection, Antiterrorism, and Illegal Immigration Control Act of 2005 (December 13, 2005), www.cbo.gov/ publication/17549; and cost estimate for H.R. 4312, the Border Security and Terrorism Prevention Act of 2005 (December 6, 2005), www.cbo.gov/publication/17539.

[50] Pew Hispanic Center, "Modes of Entry for the Unauthorized Migrant Population" (May 22, 2006), http://tinyurl.com/ korn9w9.

[51] In recent years, in addition to working with the federal government, many states have enacted their own legislation that addresses unauthorized immigration and other immigration-related policies. The strict immigration requirements enacted in Arizona in 2010 as part of the Support Our Law Enforcement and Safe Neighborhoods Act—which served as a model for legislation in other states—were challenged by the federal government. In June 2012, the Supreme Court ruled in Arizona v. United States, 132 S.Ct. 2492, that several provisions were unconstitutional.

[52] Sec. 287(g) of the Immigration and Nationality Act, 8 U.S.C. §1357(g) (2012). The program initially consisted of two components, task-force agreements and jail enforcement agreements. The task-force agreements authorized state and local law enforcement officers to identify and arrest some people on federal immigration charges as part of their regular law enforcement duties.

[53] See Congressional Budget Office, cost estimate for Senate amendment 1150 to S. 1348, the Comprehensive Immigration Reform Act of 2007 (June 2007), www.cbo.gov/publication/ 18716.

[54] See Congressional Budget Office, letter to the Honorable Patrick J. Leahy providing an estimate for S. 744, the Border Security, Economic Opportunity, and Immigration Modernization Act, as passed by the Senate on June 27, 2013 (July 3, 2013), www.cbo.gov/publication/44397.

[55] See Jeffrey S. Passel, D'Vera Cohn, and Ana Gonzales-Barrera, Net Migration From Mexico Falls to Zero—And Perhaps Less (Pew Hispanic Center, April 23, 2012), http://tinyurl.com/ cfcka2j; and Jeffrey S. Passel and D'Vera Cohn, Unauthorized Immigrants: 11.1 Million in 2011 (Pew Hispanic Center, December 6, 2012), http://tinyurl.com/m39g5wp.

[56] See Jeffrey S. Passel, D'Vera Cohn, and Molly Rohal, Unauthorized Immigrant Totals Rise in 7 States, Fall in 14 (Pew Hispanic Center, November 18, 2014), http://tinyurl.com/nf9mwzf (PDF, 2.33 MB).

[57] For an analysis of Arizona's requirement for employers to use E-verify, see, for example, Alex Nowrasteh, The Economic Case Against Arizona's Immigration Laws, Policy Analysis No. 709 (Cato Institute, September 25, 2012) http://tinyurl.com/l992jks.

[58] Data about the Employment Eligibility Verification Program provided to CBO by staff of the Citizenship and Immigration Services.

In: Immigration Policy Proposals ...
Editor: Kimberly D. Parsons
ISBN: 978-1-63482-344-9

Chapter 2

IMMIGRATION LEGISLATION AND ISSUES IN THE 113TH CONGRESS*

Andorra Bruno, Jerome P. Bjelopera, Michael John Garcia, William A. Kandel, Margaret Mikyung Lee, Alison Siskin and Ruth Ellen Wasem

SUMMARY

Immigration reform was an active legislative issue in the first session of the 113th Congress. The Senate passed the Border Security, Economic Opportunity, and Immigration Modernization Act (S.744), a comprehensive immigration reform bill that includes provisions on border security, interior enforcement, employment eligibility verification and worksite enforcement, legalization of unauthorized aliens, immigrant visas, nonimmigrant visas, and humanitarian admissions. For its part, the House took a different approach to immigration reform. Rather than considering a single comprehensive bill, the House acted on a set of immigration bills that address border security, interior enforcement, employment eligibility verification and worksite enforcement, and nonimmigrant and immigrant visas. House committees reported or ordered to be reported the following immigration bills: Border Security

---

* This is an edited, reformatted and augmented version of a Congressional Research Service publication, No. R43320, dated November 4, 2014.

Results Act of 2013 (H.R. 1417); Strengthen and Fortify Enforcement (SAFE) Act (H.R. 2278); Legal Workforce Act (H.R. 1772); Agricultural Guestworker (AG) Act (H.R. 1773); and Supplying Knowledge-based Immigrants and Lifting Levels of STEM Visas (SKILLS Visa) Act (H.R. 2131).

Beyond their work on immigration reform legislation, the House and Senate acted on other immigration-related bills. Among these measures, the 113th Congress passed the Violence Against Women Reauthorization Act of 2013 (P.L. 113-4), which includes provisions on noncitizen victims of domestic abuse or certain other crimes and on victims of human trafficking. Other immigration issues addressed in enacted measures include Iraqi and Afghan special immigrants (P.L. 113-42, P.L. 113-66, P.L. 113-76, P.L. 113-160), refugees (P.L. 113-6, P.L. 113-76), temporary nonagricultural workers (P.L. 113-76, P.L. 113-164), international adoption (P.L. 113- 74), and alien inadmissibility (P.L. 113-100).

Several bills passed one house of Congress, but not the other. In addition to the comprehensive immigration reform bill (S. 744), the Senate passed measures dealing with border security personnel compensation (S. 1691), the application of immigration law in the Commonwealth of the Northern Mariana Islands (CNMI) (S. 1237), and the visa waiver program (S. 2673). House-passed measures address, among other issues, border security and unaccompanied alien children (UAC) arriving in the United States (H.R. 5230), human trafficking (H.R. 3530, H.R. 3610, H.R. 5135), prosecutorial discretion (H.R. 2217, H.R. 5272), and the visa waiver program (H.R. 938).

This report discusses these and other immigration-related issues that received legislative action or have been of significant congressional interest in the 113th Congress.

INTRODUCTION

Immigration reform was a key issue in the first session of the 113th Congress. The Senate passed the Border Security, Economic Opportunity, and Immigration Modernization Act (S. 744), a comprehensive immigration reform bill that includes provisions on border security, interior enforcement, employment eligibility verification and worksite enforcement, legalization of unauthorized aliens, immigrant visas, nonimmigrant visas, and humanitarian admissions.[1] Taking a different approach to immigration reform, the House acted on a set of immigration bills that separately address many of the same areas of immigration policy. House Committees reported or ordered to be reported immigration bills on border security (H.R. 1417); interior enforcement (H.R. 2278); employment eligibility verification and worksite enforcement (H.R. 1772); and immigrant and nonimmigrant visas (H.R. 2131, H.R. 1773).

The House and Senate also acted on other pieces of immigration-related legislation. Among these, the Violence Against Women Reauthorization Act of 2013 (P.L. 113-4) includes provisions on noncitizen victims of domestic abuse or certain other crimes and on victims of human trafficking. The trafficking provisions address the care and custody of unaccompanied alien children (UAC), among other issues. Additionally, in response to the recent surge in arrivals of unaccompanied minors from Central America, the House-passed supplemental appropriations bill for 2014 (H.R. 5230) contains UAC-related provisions, including language that would change the procedures for screening and processing unaccompanied alien children who arrive at the U.S. border from certain countries. Many other UAC-related bills were introduced in the 113th Congress but have not seen legislative action.[2]

In addition to P.L. 113-4, the 113th Congress enacted multiple immigration-related bills. Enacted appropriations measures (P.L. 113-6, P.L. 113-76, and P.L. 113-164) variously include policy provisions on temporary nonagricultural workers, refugees, and special immigrants, among other immigration-related issues. P.L. 113-42, P.L. 113-66, and P.L. 113-160 also contain provisions on special immigrants. P.L. 113-74 concerns international adoption. P.L. 113-100 concerns inadmissibility to the United States. This report discusses these and other immigration-related issues that received legislative action or have been of significant congressional interest in the 113th Congress.[3]

BORDER SECURITY

The Department of Homeland Security (DHS) is charged with protecting U.S. borders from weapons of mass destruction, terrorists, smugglers, and unauthorized aliens. Border security involves securing the many means by which people and things can enter the country. Operationally, this means controlling the official ports of entry (POE) through which legitimate travelers and commerce enter the country, and patrolling the nation's land and maritime borders to prevent illegal entries.

DHS's U.S. Customs and Border Protection (CBP) protects 7,000 miles of U.S. international land borders with Mexico and Canada and 95,000 miles of coastal shoreline. At ports of entry, the CBP Office of Field Operations (OFO) is responsible for conducting immigration, customs, and agricultural inspections of travelers seeking admission to the United States. Between POEs, CBP's U.S. Border Patrol (USBP) is responsible for enforcing immigration law and other federal laws along the border and for preventing unlawful entries into the United States. According to USBP data, apprehensions of unauthorized migrants have declined since FY2005, reaching a 40- year low in FY2011. Although apprehensions remain at historically low levels, there have been increases since FY2011, driven by increased apprehensions of Central American families and unaccompanied alien children (UAC) at the Southwest border (see "Unaccompanied Alien Children").[4]

Border security has been an important issue for the last several Congresses. In recent years, some Members of Congress have proposed to strengthen border security as part of a "comprehensive immigration reform" bill, while others have argued that Congress should not consider other immigration reforms until the border has been secured. Debate in the 113th Congress focused primarily on border security strategy and metrics; border personnel, equipment, and infrastructure; improvements to the entry-exit system for tracking aliens' travel into and out of the United States; and DHS's access to federal lands and authority to waive certain federal laws.

Border Security Strategy and Metrics

DHS, CBP, OFO, and USBP all have published strategic plans, but they have not laid out a comprehensive operational strategy for securing U.S. borders or published clear metrics for measuring and evaluating border security.[5] The absence of such a strategy and metrics arguably has contributed to disagreements about the existing level of border security.

S. 744, as passed by the Senate, would require DHS to develop a pair of planning documents: a Comprehensive Southern Border Security Strategy and a Southern Border Fencing Strategy.[6] The bill includes a detailed list of surveillance equipment and other assets to be deployed in each Border Patrol sector along the southern border as required elements of the Comprehensive Security Strategy. It also requires that the Fencing Strategy describe plans to deploy 700 miles of southern border pedestrian fencing (up from about 352 miles of pedestrian fencing and 299 miles of vehicle barriers today). In general, the submission and implementation of the two southern border strategies are among the "triggers" that S. 744 would establish as preconditions for DHS to begin processing legalization applications for certain unauthorized aliens and to begin adjusting the status of such aliens under the bill.[7]

The goal of the Comprehensive Security Strategy would be to achieve and maintain "effective control" of all Border Patrol sectors along the southern border. Effective control would be defined to include "persistent surveillance" and at least a 90% "effectiveness rate."[8] The bill would require DHS to report to Congress biannually on implementation of the Comprehensive Security Strategy, with such reports to include sector-level effectiveness rates and information about alien recidivism (i.e., repeat apprehensions). If the DHS Secretary cannot certify that DHS has achieved effective control of all southern border sectors for at least one fiscal year within five years of the bill's passage, S. 744 would require that additional border security recommendations be issued by a Southern Border Security Commission to be composed of the governors or gubernatorial appointees from each of the southern border states (and Nevada), along with congressional and presidential appointees.

The Border Security Results Act of 2013 (H.R. 1417), as reported by the House Homeland Security Committee, would likewise require DHS to develop a Strategy to Secure the Border. H.R. 1417 differs from S. 744 in that H.R. 1417 does not describe specific assets or miles of fencing to be included in its strategy. Instead, the House bill includes an extensive list of considerations to be taken into account in the development of the strategy; and it requires that the strategy be designed to allow DHS to gain and maintain operational control of the border within deadlines established by the bill. Operational control is defined in the House bill to include at least a 90% effectiveness rate with respect to illegal border crossing as well as a "significant reduction in the movement of illegal drugs and other contraband through such areas."[9] H.R. 1417 also describes a more comprehensive set of border metrics than those identified in S. 744, including measures of illegal migration, recidivism, and drug seizures between ports of entry; measures of immigration and drug enforcement as well as crossing times at ports of entry; and immigration and drug enforcement data for maritime borders. The bill would require DHS to collaborate with outside partners in the development and review of these metrics; and it would require DHS and the Government Accountability Office (GAO) to submit regular reports to Congress indicating whether operational control of the southern border has been achieved and maintained.

Border Security Personnel, Equipment, and Infrastructure

Across a variety of indicators, the United States has substantially expanded border enforcement resources over the last three decades. Particularly since 2001, such increases have included border security personnel, fencing and infrastructure, and surveillance technology.[10]

Senate-passed S. 744 would authorize additional increases in each of these areas.[11] Under the bill, DHS would be required to more than double the number of Border Patrol agents deployed to the southern border (to 38,405, up from 18,462 in FY2013); to increase the number of CBP officers and CBP flight hours; and to deploy the specific surveillance equipment, fencing, and infrastructure assets described in the bill's border strategies (see "Border Security Strategies and Metrics").

S. 744 also would direct DHS to continuously deploy unmanned aircraft, along with other surveillance equipment, to ensure surveillance of border areas 24 hours a day, with necessary funding authorized for FY2014–FY2018. And it would support recent CBP efforts to increase the proportion of border crossers subject to criminal prosecutions and other "high consequence" enforcement outcomes by setting aside funding to triple the number of border crossing prosecutions in the Border Patrol's Tucson sector, which has accounted for the largest number of illegal crossings in recent years. The bill would support these increases with about $45 billion in direct spending on border enforcement over a 5-10 year period.[12]

The House-passed supplemental appropriations bill for 2014 (H.R. 5230) would appropriate, or otherwise make available, funds for the deployment of National Guard units and personnel to the southern border to provide support for border operations, particularly in high-traffic areas experiencing substantial crossings by unaccompanied alien children.

With respect to border security personnel compensation, S. 1691, as passed by the Senate, would create a new system for determining overtime compensation for Border Patrol agents. According to the Senate report that accompanies the bill, S. 1691 would update the Border Patrol pay system "to reflect the number of hours those agents regularly work and the way in which those hours are scheduled."[13]

Entry-Exit System

The Illegal Immigration Reform and Immigrant Responsibility Act of 1996 (P.L. 104-208, Div. C), as amended, requires DHS to maintain an automated, biometric entry-exit system that collects a record of every alien arriving to and departing from the United States. The Office of Biometric Identity Management (OBIM), formerly known as the United States Visitor and Immigration Status Indicator Technology (US-VISIT) program, is responsible for collecting and storing these data and for providing entry-exit information to other components within DHS and to other federal agencies. The entry-exit system has been a subject of ongoing congressional attention because—in spite of the mandate—DHS collects only biographic data (i.e., it does not collect biometric data) from certain visitors entering the United States, and it does not collect *any* data from certain visitors leaving the United States.[14]

Border security and immigration legislation considered in the 113th Congress would reiterate the entry-exit mandate, with a particular focus on further development of the exit tracking system. In the House, committee-reported H.R. 1417 would require DHS, within 180 days of the bill's enactment, to submit a plan to Congress to implement immediately a biometric exit system at U.S. ports of entry, or to submit alternative plans that would achieve the same level of security within two years if DHS determines that a biometric exit system is not feasible. And the Strengthen and Fortify Enforcement (SAFE) Act (H.R. 2278), as ordered to be reported by the House Judiciary Committee, would require that DHS establish a biometric entry-exit system within two years of the bill's enactment.

Senate-passed S. 744 would impose a new exit-tracking requirement by making air and sea carriers responsible for collecting machine-readable passport data and other travel information from departing passengers, and for transmitting such data to DHS. (Air and sea carriers currently submit passenger manifest data to DHS.) DHS also would be required, within two years of enactment, to establish a biometric exit system at the 10 U.S. airports with the greatest volume of international travel. Following a report to Congress, DHS would be required to expand biometric data collection to 30 airports and to develop a plan for such data collection at major land and sea ports. S. 744 would further require that DHS ensure that "reasonably available enforcement resources are employed" to locate and remove visa overstays identified by the entry-exit system,[15] and that at least 90% of people who enter the United States after the bill's enactment and who overstay their visas by more than 180 days are placed in removal proceedings or otherwise have their cases resolved.

Access to Federal Lands and DHS Waiver Authority

Access to Federal Lands

More than 40% of the southern border abuts federal and tribal lands overseen by the Department of Agriculture (USDA) or the Department of the Interior (DOI), including some areas that have been identified as "high-risk areas" for marijuana smuggling and illegal migration.[16] DHS is not the lead law enforcement agency on USDA and DOI lands, but the three departments have signed Memoranda of Understanding (MOUs) concerning information sharing with respect to border security and DHS access to these lands. Some Members of Congress have argued that DHS should have more complete access to public lands for law enforcement purposes, though Border Patrol officials have testified that existing MOUs allow USBP to carry out its border security mission.[17]

Legislation considered in the 113th Congress would broaden DHS authority on such lands. Senate-passed S. 744 would require USDA and DOI to provide CBP personnel with immediate access to federal lands within Arizona for certain security activities. CBP would be required to conduct its activities, to the maximum extent possible, in a manner that the DHS Secretary determines will best protect natural and cultural resources when acting on federal lands and to prepare an environmental impact statement in connection with its enforcement efforts. More broadly, both House-passed H.R. 5230 and H.R. 2278, as ordered to be reported by the House Judiciary Committee, would give DHS immediate access to USDA and DOI lands within 100 miles of international land borders; and it would explicitly prohibit USDA or DOI from impeding or restricting CBP's border security activities on such lands.

DHS Waiver Authority

In general, federal agencies are required to review the potential impact of proposed projects on natural and cultural resources prior to committing resources to a project.[18] These environmental and other review requirements may delay the construction of certain border infrastructure; but existing law grants DHS broad authority to waive legal requirements that might delay construction of border barriers.[19]

Senate-passed S. 744 would grant the DHS Secretary authority to waive any law, as the Secretary deems necessary, to ensure expeditious construction of barriers, roads, and other infrastructure to secure the southern border. This provision potentially applies to a broader range of border infrastructure projects than the waiver authority in current law, but only applies to projects along the southern border.[20] The waiver authority would terminate upon certification by DHS that the bill's border fencing and border security strategies have been substantially implemented (see "Border Security Strategies and Metrics"). Both House-passed H.R. 5230 and H.R. 2278, as ordered to be reported by the House Judiciary Committee, would also exempt application of specific laws (previously waived by the Secretary of DHS in 2008 with respect to certain border construction projects) to CBP border construction projects on all federal lands under DOI and USDA jurisdiction within 100 miles of U.S. international land borders.[21]

INTERIOR ENFORCEMENT

In addition to establishing a comprehensive set of rules governing the admission, continued presence, and departure of foreign nationals, the Immigration and Nationality Act (INA) [22] establishes an enforcement regime to deter violations of federal immigration law. Some violations are subject to civil monetary penalties; other violations may be subject to criminal fines and imprisonment; and still others, if committed by an alien, may be grounds for denying the alien admission into the country, removing the alien from the United States, or making the alien ineligible for certain immigration benefits or relief from removal.

Legislative proposals in the 113th Congress, including H.R. 2278, as ordered to be reported by the House Judiciary Committee, and Senate-passed S. 744, would modify the INA's enforcement provisions applicable to persons found within the United States ("interior enforcement" provisions). Both bills would heighten criminal penalties associated with violations of federal immigration law and establish new grounds for inadmissibility and deportability. The bills differ in several important ways, however, with H.R. 2278 generally imposing more significant penalties for immigration-related violations and more stringent requirements relating to the detention and removal of aliens than S. 744. H.R. 2278 also contains provisions encouraging states and localities to play a more active role in immigration enforcement.

Criminal Sanctions

S. 744 and H.R. 2278 would make numerous changes to existing immigration-related criminal offenses. Among other things,[23] both bills would amend existing criminal statutes concerning passport and immigration-related document fraud, along with the criminal prohibitions on the smuggling and harboring of unauthorized aliens. In each case, the modifications would generally involve widening the scope of proscribed conduct and heightening the available criminal penalties,[24] at least when certain aggravating circumstances exist.

Both bills would revise the criminal statutes addressing unlawful entry by an alien[25] and unlawful reentry of an alien in violation of an outstanding order of removal,[26] including by increasing available penalties in certain circumstances. H.R. 2278 would expand the scope of the unlawful entry and reentry statutes to expressly cover illegal border crossings, regardless of whether a crossing occurred while the alien was under surveillance by immigration authorities. S. 744 would establish a new criminal offense for hindering or obstructing the apprehension of aliens unlawfully entering the United States. S. 744 would also eliminate current criminal penalties associated with *attempting* to unlawfully enter the country. In addition, the Senate bill would provide an affirmative defense to an alien criminally charged with unlawful reentry into the country in violation of an outstanding removal order, if the alien had been removed from the country while a minor, and would exempt from criminal liability certain reentry offenses that involve the provision of emergency humanitarian assistance.

H.R. 2278 would make unlawful alien presence a criminal offense. Specifically, the bill would make it a crime for an alien to either (1) knowingly violate the terms of his admission or parole or (2) otherwise knowingly be unlawfully present in the country for any period of time. Criminal liability would not attach to periods of unlawful presence as a minor or generally to unauthorized aliens with bona fide pending asylum applications, battered women or children, or victims of severe forms of trafficking.

Inadmissibility, Deportability, and Relief from Removal

The INA provides that aliens who engage in specified activities, including various forms of criminal conduct and activities posing a threat to U.S. security (e.g., terrorism), are generally barred from admission and subject to removal.[27] Some forms of conduct may also make an alien ineligible for many forms of relief from removal (e.g., asylum). The most significant immigration consequences typically attach to aliens convicted of any offense defined as an "aggravated felony" by the INA.[28]

Both S. 744 and H.R. 2278 would add new grounds for alien inadmissibility and/or deportability.[29] For example, both bills include provisions making aliens who commit certain fraud-related offenses or who are involved with criminal street gangs inadmissible or deportable; and modify the grounds of inadmissibility to cover crimes of domestic violence, child abuse, stalking, and violation of protection orders (all of which are already grounds for deportability). Both bills contain provisions concerning the removability of aliens convicted of multiple driving under the influence (DUI) offenses. S. 744 would add or expand existing grounds of inadmissibility relating to the withholding of information for biometric screening and severe human rights violations. H.R. 2278 would amend the grounds of inadmissibility to expressly cover aggravated felony convictions (already a ground for deportability) and additional firearms offenses. Both H.R. 2278 and S. 744 would authorize immigration authorities, in certain circumstances, to consider evidence that is extrinsic to the conviction record when determining whether an alien engaged in conduct making him or her removable under specified grounds.

Both bills would also make changes to the INA's definition of aggravated felony, with H.R. 2278 making the more substantial modifications. Among other things, the House bill would designate as aggravated felonies, criminal convictions for unlawful entry, presence, or reentry, as long as the length of imprisonment for the offense is at least a year. Both H.R. 2278 and S. 744 would also designate DUI convictions as aggravated felonies in certain circumstances.

S. 744 would increase immigration authorities' discretion to waive certain grounds of inadmissibility. Among other things, it would give immigration judges discretion to not order certain aliens in removal proceedings to be removed, deported, or excluded if the judge determines that such actions would be against the public interest, would create a hardship to the alien's U.S. citizen or permanent resident immediate relatives, or if the alien appears eligible for naturalization. This waiver would not be available to individuals who are inadmissible or deportable based on certain criminal and national security grounds. The Secretary of DHS would have similar discretion to waive grounds of inadmissibility.

H.R. 2278 would modify the immigration consequences for some types of criminal activity. For example, it would prohibit refugees and asylees who have committed aggravated felonies from obtaining legal permanent residence. It would make aliens who are removable due to involvement with criminal street gangs or who are described in the terrorism-related grounds for inadmissibility or removal, ineligible for many forms of relief from removal. H.R. 2278 also would make streamlined removal proceedings potentially applicable to a broader category of criminal aliens. House-passed H.R. 5230 would make ineligible for asylum those aliens believed to have committed, prior to their arrival in the United States, a drug-related offense punishable by more than one year's imprisonment.

P.L. 113-100 directs the President to deny admission to a person seeking to enter the United States as a representative to the United Nations if it is determined that the person has engaged in terrorist activity against the United States or its allies. This provision may be waived if the President deems it to be in the national security interests of the United States.

The House-passed defense authorization bill for 2015 (H.R. 4435) and the competing Senate version that was reported by the Senate Committee on Armed Services (S. 2410) contain provisions that would limit the application of the INA's terrorism-related provisions to the Kurdistan Democratic Party and the Patriotic Union of Kurdistan.

Detention of Aliens

Under the INA, individual aliens placed in removal proceedings are potentially subject to detention, but could also be released on parole or bond.[30] Certain categories of aliens, however, are subject to mandatory detention during removal proceedings.[31] The INA also contains provisions concerning the detention of aliens ordered removed until such time as their removal may be effectuated.

S. 744 contains provisions that appear intended to reduce the number of aliens held in DHS custody throughout removal proceedings. For example, under S. 744, except in the cases of certain terrorists and criminal aliens, detention would be required only if the Secretary of DHS demonstrates that no conditions, including the use of alternatives to detention that maintain custody over the alien, would reasonably assure the appearance of the alien at immigration proceedings and the safety of any other person. The bill would also generally require determinations by immigration judges as to whether an alien's continued detention is warranted. For aliens not eligible for bail or to be released on recognizance, another provision of S. 744 would require DHS to establish a secure alternatives program offering a "continuum of supervision mechanisms and options."[32] Most aliens, including many who are subject to mandatory detention, would potentially be eligible for the secure alternatives program.

H.R. 2278, in contrast, would seek to augment immigration authorities' ability to detain aliens identified for removal until their removal may be effectuated. Some provisions seek to ensure that certain categories of aliens—particularly those involved in criminal activity or deemed to pose a threat to the community—remain detained throughout the removal process and until removed. Other provisions of the bill would make unlawfully present aliens convicted of one or more DUI offenses and aliens removable on account of involvement with criminal street gangs subject to mandatory detention during removal. Other provisions would establish detention requirements that are more generally applicable to any alien placed in removal proceedings or ordered removed.

Prosecutorial or Enforcement Discretion

The Obama Administration has issued several documents that provide guidance regarding the exercise of prosecutorial discretion in immigration enforcement activities. In so doing, it has emphasized that the exercise of discretion in individual cases is appropriate to "ensure that agency resources are focused on our enforcement priorities, including individuals who pose a threat to public safety, are recent border crossers, or repeatedly violate our immigration laws."[33] The Administration has also claimed that the exercise of such discretion can promote humanitarian interests. Others, however, have suggested that the Administration's prosecutorial discretion policies are tantamount to "amnesty," and that the Deferred Action for Childhood Arrivals (DACA) initiative,[34] in particular, contravenes certain provisions of the INA.[35]

H.R. 2278, as ordered to be reported by the House Judiciary Committee, contains provisions that would respond to the Obama Administration's initiatives, apparently with the intent of foreclosing certain exercises of prosecutorial discretion and promoting more vigorous enforcement of federal immigration law. The bill would require annual reports on exercises of prosecutorial discretion. It would also bar DHS from finalizing, implementing, administering, or enforcing recent guidance regarding prosecutorial discretion, including DACA. A similar restriction is contained in the House-passed version of H.R. 2217, the Department of Homeland Security Appropriations Act, 2014. House-passed H.R. 5272 would bar federal funds from being used to consider any new or previously adjudicated DACA application; authorize deferred action for any class of unlawfully present aliens; or provide work authorization to any alien not lawfully admitted into the country who is not in lawful immigration status on the bill's date of enactment.

As previously discussed, S. 744 would provide statutory authorization to DHS and immigration judges to exercise discretion in a broader range of cases involving removable aliens (see "Grounds of Inadmissibility and Deportability and Relief from Removal").

State and Local Involvement in Immigration Enforcement

The role that states and localities play in enforcing federal immigration law has been a topic of significant interest in recent years.[36] Some states and localities, concerned about what they perceive as inadequate federal enforcement of immigration law, have sought to independently enforce federal law, as well as to penalize conduct that may facilitate the presence of unauthorized aliens within their jurisdiction. Other states and localities, in contrast, have proscribed activities (e.g., sharing information, honoring federal requests to hold aliens) that could assist in federal immigration enforcement because they maintain that the federal government has been too aggressive in removing aliens who are not criminals and have ties to the community.

At least until 2012, there had been considerable debate regarding the ability of states and local officers to independently act to enforce federal immigration law, or to impose criminal sanctions upon activities that facilitate unauthorized immigration, separate and apart from any sanctions imposed under federal law. In its decision in the case of *Arizona v. United States*, however, the Supreme Court found that existing federal law contemplates states and localities having a limited role in immigration enforcement.[37] The Court indicated that states' ability to criminally sanction immigration-related activities is limited, even when these sanctions mirror those of the federal government. The Court also ruled that states generally cannot arrest aliens on the basis of suspected removability except with express federal statutory authorization or pursuant to the request, approval, or instruction of federal immigration authorities.

H.R. 2278 includes several provisions that seem intended to override aspects of the Supreme Court's ruling in *Arizona* and provide states and localities with express statutory authorization to engage in immigration enforcement activities. Among other things, H.R. 2278 would authorize states and localities to arrest and transfer removable aliens to federal immigration authorities' custody and permit states and localities to impose their own criminal penalties for conduct constituting a criminal offense under federal immigration law. Other provisions would require greater information sharing by federal, state, and local authorities for immigration purposes; encourage the continuation and expansion of cooperative arrangements with states or localities on immigration enforcement matters, including through written agreements under INA §287(g);[38] and require that DHS consider assuming custody of removable aliens in state or local custody if requested to do so. The bill would also condition certain federal funding for states and localities upon their cooperation in enforcing federal immigration law.

EMPLOYMENT ELIGIBILITY VERIFICATION AND WORKSITE ENFORCEMENT

Employment eligibility verification and worksite enforcement (one component of interior enforcement) are widely viewed as essential elements of a strategy to reduce unauthorized immigration. Under §274A of the INA, it is unlawful for an employer to knowingly hire, recruit or refer for a fee, or continue to employ an alien who is not authorized to be so employed. Employers are further required to participate in a paper-based (I-9) employment eligibility verification system in which they examine documents presented by new hires to verify identity and work eligibility, and to complete and retain I-9 verification forms. Employers violating prohibitions on unlawful employment may be subject to civil and/or criminal penalties. Enforcement of these provisions, termed "worksite enforcement," is the responsibility of DHS's U.S. Immigration and Customs Enforcement (ICE).

While all employers must meet the I-9 requirements, they may also elect to participate in the E-Verify electronic employment eligibility verification system.[39] E-Verify is administered by DHS's U.S. Citizenship and Immigration Services (USCIS). Participants in E-Verify electronically verify new hires' employment authorization through Social Security Administration

(SSA) and, if necessary, DHS databases.[40] E-Verify is a temporary program, currently authorized through September 30, 2015.

Several bills on electronic employment eligibility verification have been introduced in the 113th Congress.[41] Two measures have seen legislative action. The House Judiciary Committee has ordered to be reported the Legal Workforce Act (H.R. 1772). S. 744, as passed by the Senate, includes provisions on employment eligibility verification and worksite enforcement in Title III. Both bills would amend the INA to permanently authorize a new electronic verification system modeled on E-Verify. Under both bills, an employer, after reviewing employee documents evidencing identity and employment authorization and completing a verification form with the employee, would seek confirmation of the employee-provided information through the electronic verification system.

The new electronic verification system proposed in H.R. 1772 would be mandatory for all employers in cases of hiring, recruitment, and referral. The verification requirements with respect to hiring would be phased in by employer size, with the largest employers (those with 10,000 or more employees) required to participate six months after the date of enactment and the smallest employers (those with less than 20 employees) required to participate two years after the date of enactment. The requirements with respect to recruitment and referral would apply one year after the date of enactment. The bill also would provide for mandatory reverification of workers with temporary work authorization, which would be phased in on the same schedule as the verification requirements for hiring. Special provisions would apply to agriculture; the hiring, recruitment and referral, and reverification provisions would not apply to agricultural workers until two years after the date of enactment. Prior to these phase-in dates, existing requirements to use E-Verify would remain in effect.

H.R. 1772 would require or permit electronic verification in ways not currently allowed under E-Verify. Employers could conduct electronic verification after making an offer of employment but before hiring, and could condition a job offer on final verification under the system. Verification of previously hired individuals would be mandatory in some cases (such as, federal, state, and local government employees). DHS could authorize or direct a critical infrastructure employer to use the system to the extent DHS determines is necessary for critical infrastructure protection. In addition, employers could verify current employees on a voluntary basis.

H.R. 1772 would significantly increase existing civil and criminal penalties for violations of the revised INA §274A prohibitions on unauthorized employment and for violations of requirements to conduct verification. It would establish as violations of the prohibition on unauthorized employment, the failure to seek electronic verification as required or the knowing provision of false information to the electronic system. H.R. 1772 would provide for the blocking of social security numbers from use in the verification system in cases of misuse and in other specified circumstances. It also would enable individuals to limit use of their social security numbers or other information for verification purposes.

In addition, H.R. 1772 includes language to expressly preempt any state or local law that relates to the hiring, employment, or verification of the employment eligibility of unauthorized aliens. At the same time, a state or locality could exercise its authority over business licensing and similar laws as a penalty for failure to use the verification system and a state, at its own expense, could enforce the revised INA §274A provisions, under specified terms. The bill also would require DHS to establish an office to receive complaints from state and local agencies about potential violations.

Among its other provisions, H.R. 1772 would direct DHS to establish an Identity Authentication Employment Eligibility Pilot Program, which would "provide for identity authentication and employment eligibility verification with respect to enrolled new employees."[42] The Senate bill, as discussed below, would mandate the use of an identity authentication mechanism.

Like H.R. 1772, Senate-passed S. 744 would amend the INA to authorize a new Electronic Verification System (EVS) modeled on E-Verify, through which employers would seek confirmation of employee-provided information. Employers also would be required to use a new identity authentication mechanism to be developed by DHS to verify the identity of each individual an employer seeks to hire. For certain documents, the mechanism would consist of a "photo tool" to enable an employer to compare the photograph on a document provided by an individual to the original image on that same document.[43]

Under S. 744, the EVS would be mandatory for all employers in cases of hiring, recruitment, and referral for a fee. Employers also would have to reverify the employment authorized status of individuals with temporary work authorization. As under H.R. 1772, the verification requirements would be phased in, but on a different timetable. All federal agencies would be required to participate in the EVS on the earlier of the date of enactment, to the extent each agency is required to participate in E-Verify and as already implemented, or 90 days after the date of enactment. Federal contractors would be required to participate in the EVS in accordance with current regulatory requirements to participate in E-Verify. Beginning one year after implementing regulations are published,[44] DHS could direct any employer involved in critical infrastructure to participate in the EVS to the extent the Secretary determines such participation would assist in critical infrastructure protection; these employers could be required to participate in the EVS with respect to newly hired employees as well as current workers.

The phase-in of the EVS participation requirements for other employers with respect to newly hired employees and employees with expiring employment authorization documents would begin no later than two years after the publication of implementing regulations (for employers with more than 5,000 employees) and would end no later than five years after the publication of implementing regulations (for the last group, tribal government employers). Agricultural employers would be required to participate in the EVS no later than four years after regulations are published.[45]

DHS would be directed to develop procedures to provide individuals with direct access to their case histories in the EVS, and to notify them of queries and EVS responses. S. 744 would establish processes for an individual to seek administrative review and judicial review of a final nonconfirmation. The bill would enable individuals to limit the use of their social security numbers or other information for verification purposes. In addition, S. 744 would provide for regular privacy and accuracy audits and civil rights assessments of the EVS.

With respect to enforcement, S. 744 would direct DHS to establish procedures for the filing and investigation of unlawful employment-related complaints by individuals and entities. Like H.R. 1772, the Senate bill would significantly increase existing civil and criminal penalties for violations of the revised INA §274A prohibitions on unauthorized employment and for violations of requirements to conduct verification. An employer who hires a worker without using the electronic system when required to do so would be presumed to have violated the §274A prohibitions on unauthorized employment. Among the new penalties S. 744 would create, DHS would be authorized to establish an "enhanced civil penalty" in cases in which an employer both fails to use the EVS and violates a federal, state, or local law on the payment of wages, work hours, or workplace health and safety.

Like H.R. 1772, S. 744 includes language to expressly preempt any state or local law that relates to the hiring, employment, or verification of the employment eligibility of unauthorized aliens, though a state may exercise its authority over business licensing or similar laws to impose penalties for failure to use the federal employment verification system. Unlike H.R. 1772, however, it does not make provision for state enforcement of the INA §274A provisions on unauthorized employment.[46]

VISA SECURITY

The Department of State (DOS) and DHS both play key roles in administering the law and policies on the admission of aliens to the United States. All foreign nationals seeking visas (see "Temporary Admissions," "Permanent Admissions") must undergo admissibility reviews performed by DOS consular officers abroad. These reviews are intended to ensure that applicants are not ineligible for admission to the United States under the grounds for inadmissibility spelled out in INA §212. These criteria include health-related grounds, criminal history, security and terrorist concerns, public charge (e.g., indigence), and previous immigration offenses.[47]

Consular officers use the Consular Consolidated Database (CCD) to screen visa applicants. Records of all visa applications are now automated in the CCD, with some records dating back to the mid-1990s. Since February 2001, the CCD has stored photographs of all visa applicants in electronic form, and the CCD has stored 10-finger scans since 2007. In addition to indicating the outcome of any prior visa application and comments by consular officers, the system links to other security databases to flag problems that may have an impact on the issuance of the visa.

Although DOS's Consular Affairs is responsible for issuing visas, DHS agencies perform related functions.[48] There was discussion of assigning all visa issuance responsibilities to DHS when the department was being created, but the Homeland Security Act of 2002 (HSA, P.L. 107-296) drew on compromise language stating that DHS would issue regulations regarding visa issuances, and that DOS would continue to issue visas. The question of which agency should take the lead in visa issuances continues to be debated.

Along these lines, Title IV of H.R. 2278, as ordered to be reported by the House Committee on the Judiciary, would give the Secretary of Homeland Security "exclusive authority to issue regulations, establish policy, and administer and enforce the provisions of the [INA] and all other immigration or nationality laws relating to the functions of consular officers of the United States in connection with the granting and refusal of a visa." The bill would broaden the exception to the confidentiality requirement relating to the sharing of information with foreign governments, including by allowing such sharing for purposes of "determining a person's deportability or eligibility for a visa, admission, or other immigration benefit," or any other instance when "the Secretary of State determines that it is in the national interest."[49] H.R. 2278 would narrow DOS's authority to waive personal interviews for visa applicants and would add national security and "high risk of degradation of visa program integrity" as reasons for requiring a personal interview.[50] The legislation would also give consular officers the authority *not* to interview visa applicants deemed to be ineligible for the visas they are seeking. In addition, H.R. 2278 would give DHS the authority to refuse or revoke any visa to any alien or class of aliens if the Secretary determines that such refusal or revocation is necessary or advisable in the security interests of the United States.[51]

Some in Congress have been particularly interested in the Visa Security Program (VSP), which the ICE Office of International Affairs (OIA) operates in certain high-risk consular posts. As described by DHS, the VSP sends ICE special agents with expertise in immigration law and counterterrorism to foreign consulates, where they perform visa security activities that complement the DOS visa screening process. According to DHS, the VSP provides law enforcement resources not available to consular officers. One of the major tasks for VSP agents is to screen visa applicants to determine their risk profiles. GAO, however, released an evaluation of the VSP that identified several shortcomings. In addition to noting that tensions exist between consular officials and VSP agents, GAO was especially concerned about the lack of standard operating procedures for VSP agents across the various posts. Most importantly, perhaps, GAO stated that ICE has not expanded the VSP to key high-risk posts despite well-publicized plans to do so.[52]

H.R. 2278 would seek to expand the VSP by requiring DHS to conduct an on-site review of all visa applications and supporting documentation before adjudication, at the top 30 visa-issuing posts designated jointly by the Secretaries of State and Homeland Security as high-risk posts. It further would call for expedited clearance and placement of DHS personnel at overseas embassies and consular posts.

Temporary Admissions

Nonimmigrants—such as tourists, foreign students, diplomats, temporary workers, cultural exchange participants, or intracompany business personnel—are admitted to the United States for a specific purpose and a temporary period of time. Nonimmigrants are required to leave the country when their visas expire, though certain classes of nonimmigrants are "dual intent," meaning that they may maintain nonimmigrant status while, at the same time, seeking to adjust to lawful permanent resident (LPR) status[53] if they otherwise qualify. Current law describes 24 major nonimmigrant visa categories, and over 70 specific types of nonimmigrant visas, which are often referred to by the letter that denotes their section in the statute, such as H-2A agricultural workers, F-1 foreign students, or J-1 cultural exchange visitors.[54]

High-Skilled Temporary Workers

The 113th Congress considered legislation that would make extensive revisions to nonimmigrant categories for professional specialty workers (H-1B visas), intra-company transferees (L visas), and other skilled temporary workers. S. 744, as passed by the Senate, and the Supplying Knowledge-based Immigrants and Lifting Levels of STEM Visas Act (SKILLS Visa Act; H.R. 2131), as ordered to be reported by the House Committee on the Judiciary, would substantially revise these visa categories.

H-1B Professional Specialty Workers

Current law makes H-1B visas available for professional specialty workers. H-1B visas are good for three years, renewable once; and they are "dual intent," meaning aliens on H-1B visas may seek LPR status while maintaining H-1B status in the United States. Current law generally limits annual H-1B admissions to 65,000, but most H-1B workers are admitted outside the cap because they are returning workers and are, therefore, exempt from the cap or they work for universities and nonprofit research facilities that are exempt from the cap.

Employers seeking to hire an H-1B worker must attest that the employer will pay the nonimmigrant the greater of the actual wages paid to other employees in the same job or the prevailing wages for that occupation; working conditions for the nonimmigrant will not adversely affect U.S. workers; and there is no applicable strike or lockout. The employer must provide a copy of the labor attestation to representatives of the bargaining unit where applicable, or must post the labor attestation in conspicuous locations at the work site. Prospective H-1B nonimmigrants must demonstrate to USCIS that they have the requisite education and work experience for the posted positions.[55]

Both S. 744 and H.R. 2131 would seek to address perceived H-1B shortages by increasing the annual numerical limits. S. 744 would replace the 65,000 per year cap on new H-1B admissions with a flexible cap that would range from a floor of 115,000 to a ceiling of 180,000 annually, with a "market-based" mechanism to increase or decrease the cap based on demand during the previous year (i.e., whether and how quickly the previous year's limit was reached). Under S. 744, up to 25,000 visas would be exempted from the cap for foreign nationals with graduate degrees in a science, technology, engineering, or mathematics (STEM) field. H.R. 2131 would raise the cap to 155,000 and would include an additional 40,000 H-1B visas for STEM graduates with masters' or doctoral degrees. Both bills would permit spouses of H-1B workers to work.

S. 744 would seek to protect U.S. workers by modifying H-1B application requirements and procedures for investigating H-1B complaints. The bill would amend the H-1B labor certification process to revise wage requirements based on Department of Labor (DOL) surveys, and would require employers to advertise for U.S. workers on a DOL website. S. 744 also would broaden DOL's authority to investigate alleged employer violations, would require DOL to conduct annual compliance audits of certain employers, and would increase DOL reporting requirements and information sharing between DOL and USCIS. Both S. 744 and H.R. 2131 would revise the prevailing wage schedules. H.R. 2131 would give DOL subpoena powers in an attempt to assure employer compliance with the H-1B rules.

L Visa Intra-Company Transferees

Current law permits certain workers to enter the United States on nonimmigrant L visas as intracompany transferees. The L visa is designed for executives, managers, and employees with specialized knowledge of a firm's products. It permits multinational firms to transfer top-level personnel to their locations in the United States for up to five to seven years.[56] Some Members of Congress have raised concerns that the L visa may result in displacement of U.S. workers employed in those positions. L workers are often comparable in skills and occupations to H-1B workers, but the L visa is not subject to the labor market attestation requirements the law sets for hiring H-1B workers. These concerns have been raised, in particular, with respect to certain outsourcing and information technology firms that employ L workers as subcontractors within the United States.

S. 744 would add prohibitions on the outsourcing and outplacement of L employees. Employers seeking to bring an L visa worker to the United States to open a new office would face special application requirements. DHS would be required to work with DOS to verify the existence of multinational companies petitioning for the L workers. With respect to compliance, DHS would be authorized to investigate and adjudicate alleged employer violations of L visa program requirements for up to 24 months after the alleged violation; and DOL would be required to conduct annual compliance audits of certain employers.

H.R. 2131 would add new labor market conditions to the INA pertaining to L petitions. The bill would require employers of certain L workers who will be working a cumulative period of six months over a three-year period to pay either the actual wage paid to similarly employed workers or the prevailing wage, whichever is higher. Under H.R. 2131, the employer would have to provide working conditions that will not adversely affect working conditions of similarly employed workers.

Other Skilled and Professional Workers

Current law includes two nonimmigrant visa categories similar to H-1B visas for temporary professional workers from specific countries: North American Free Trade Agreement (NAFTA) TN visas for Canadian and Mexican temporary professional workers, and E-3 treaty professional visas for Australians. Among the related provisions in legislation that received action in the 113th Congress, S. 744 would create a new category for specialty workers from countries with whom the United States has signed a free trade agreement. H.R. 2131 would extend the required $500 fee for H-1B visa and L visa fraud detection and prevention programs to employers of TN, E-3, and certain H-1B workers.

Several other employment-based nonimmigrant visas are intended to attract outstanding individuals, entrepreneurs, professionals, and high-skilled workers. Among these visas is the O visa for persons with outstanding and extraordinary ability. S. 744 and H.R. 2131 would add visa portability for foreign nationals on O-1 visas, enabling them to change employers, and would add flexibility to the requirements for being admitted on an O-1 visa based on achievement in motion picture or television production.

S. 744 would significantly amend the E-1 and E-2 visa categories for treaty traders and treaty investors from countries with whom the United States has signed a treaty of commerce and navigation.[57] Although more than 70 countries are eligible for these visas, the United States no longer enters into treaties of commerce and navigation. Among other changes, S. 744 would allow E visas to be issued to citizens of countries where there is a bilateral investment treaty or a free trade agreement.[58] In addition, the Senate bill would create a new nonimmigrant X visa for qualified entrepreneurs whose U.S. business entities meet certain requirements regarding attracting investment, or generating revenues and creating jobs. None of the House bills that have seen committee action contain similar provisions, but H.R. 2131 would create a pathway for E-2s to become LPRs (see "Investor Visas").[59]

Lower-Skilled Temporary Workers

Under current law, lower-skilled temporary workers (sometimes referred to as guest workers) can enter the United States on H-2A agricultural worker visas and H-2B nonagricultural worker visas to perform temporary or seasonal work. Bringing in an H-2A or H-2B worker is a multi-agency, multi-step process. Among the required steps, employers must apply to the Department of Labor for a certification that there are not sufficient U.S. workers who are qualified and available to perform the work; and that the employment of foreign workers will not adversely affect the wages and working conditions of U.S. workers who are similarly employed. Before filing such a labor certification application with DOL, prospective H-2A and H-2B employers must attempt to recruit U.S. workers. As part of the labor certification process, employers must offer and provide required wages and benefits to guest workers and similarly employed U.S. workers.[60] Senate and House bills that have received action in the 113th Congress variously contain provisions on lower-skilled temporary workers.

Agricultural Guest Workers

S. 744, as passed by the Senate, and the Agricultural Guest Worker Act, or the AG Act (H.R. 1773), as ordered to be reported by the House Judiciary Committee, would establish new temporary agricultural worker visas. S. 744 would establish new W-3 and W-4 nonimmigrant visas for agricultural workers, and H.R. 1773 would create a new H-2C nonimmigrant agricultural worker visa.

While the new agricultural worker visas proposed in the Senate and the House measures differ, they share some similarities that distinguish them from the existing H-2A visa. Both the Senate and the House bills would sunset the H-2A visa program. Among the new features of the Senate-proposed and the House-proposed replacement agricultural worker visa programs, these visas, unlike the H-2A visa, would not be limited to temporary or seasonal agricultural work and would not require prospective employers to apply for DOL labor certification or to meet all existing certification requirements. Both new programs also would provide for at-will employment by agricultural workers. In addition, both the Senate and the House agricultural worker proposals include provisions to enable certain unauthorized aliens to obtain legal temporary or permanent immigration status.[61]

Nonagricultural Guest Workers

S. 744, as passed by the Senate, would make changes to the H-2B visa. Current law permits the admission of H-2B visa holders to perform temporary, non-agricultural work when sufficient qualified U.S. workers are not available. H-2B visas are subject to a statutory cap of 66,000 visas per year. S. 744 would provide for the admission of additional H-2B workers outside the statutory cap, while also imposing additional requirements on H-2B employers. Among these provisions, S. 744 would renew an H-2B returning worker exemption from the annual cap that was in effect in FY2005-FY2007 and provide that H-2B nonimmigrants counted toward the H-2B cap for FY2013 would not be counted again for FY2014 through FY2018.

In addition to revising the H-2B visa, S. 744 would create a new W-1 visa for nonagricultural temporary workers and a new W-2 visa for the spouses and children of such workers. Unlike the H-2B visa, the W-1 visa would not be limited to temporary or seasonal work and would not require prospective employers to apply for DOL labor certification. More generally, the W-1 visa would be subject to a different set of requirements than the H-2B visa. W-1 nonimmigrants would be admitted to work in registered positions, which would be limited to lower-skilled occupations and generally to metropolitan areas where the unemployment rate is 8.5% or less. The number of positions would range from 20,000 to 200,000 per year, to be determined as specified in S. 744. Additional positions could be created for shortage occupations and as special allocations for certain employers who meet specified recruitment requirements. W-2 nonimmigrants also would be authorized to work in the United States.[62]

An H-2B provision was enacted as part of the Consolidated Appropriations Act, 2014 (P.L. 113- 76). It allows an employer in the seafood industry with an approved H-2B petition to bring in H-2B workers at any time during the 120-day period beginning on the employer's stated date of need for workers, without filing another petition. This provision, which was initially in effect until September 30, 2014, has been extended until December 11, 2014, by the Continuing Appropriations Resolution, 2015 (P.L. 113-164 §140).

Other Temporary Admissions

The 113th Congress also considered changes to the temporary visa categories for foreign visitors to the United States and foreign students.

Tourists

There has been longstanding interest in Congress in promoting international tourism to the United States. S. 744 would allow Canadians over age 55 entering on B tourist visas who own or have rented property in the United States to be admitted for a period not to exceed 240 days. Currently, the maximum admission time on a B visa is 180 days.[63] S. 744 would also create a new nonimmigrant visa category (Y) for those over 55 years of age who own property in the United States.[64] Similar provisions are contained in the Jobs Originated through Launching Travel (JOLT) Act of 2013 (H.R. 1354).

Visa Waiver Program

The Visa Waiver Program (VWP) allows nationals from certain countries to enter the United States as temporary visitors for business or pleasure without first obtaining a visa from a U.S. consulate abroad.[65] Aliens entering under the VWP must get approval from the Electronic System for Travel Authorization (ESTA), a web-based system that checks the alien's information against relevant law enforcement and security databases, before they can board a plane to the United States. To qualify for the VWP, the INA specifies that a country must: offer reciprocal privileges to U.S. citizens; have had a nonimmigrant refusal rate[66] of less than 3% for the previous year; issue their nationals machine-readable passports that incorporate biometric identifiers (see "Entry-Exit System"); certify that it is developing a program to issue tamper-resistant, machine-readable visa documents that incorporate biometric identifiers which are verifiable at the country's port of entry; and not compromise the law enforcement or security interests of the United States by its inclusion in the program.

Senate-passed S. 744 would make several changes to the VWP, including authorizing the Secretary of DHS, in consultation with the Secretary of State, to designate a country as a VWP country if the country's nonimmigrant refusal rate and/or nonimmigrant overstay rate[67] was less than 3% in the previous fiscal year.[68] As indicated above, only the refusal rate is currently used in deciding whether a country should be in the VWP. S. 744 would also allow the Secretary of DHS to waive the refusal rate requirement if certain conditions are met.[69] In addition, the bill would revise the current probationary period and procedures for terminating a country's participation in the VWP if that country fails to comply with any of the program's requirements.[70]

In 2009, Congress created the Corporation for Travel Promotion (called Brand USA), a public-private entity to promote U.S. tourism that is funded by a $10 travel promotion fee levied against ESTA applicants.[71] By statute, the travel promotion fee expires at the end of FY2015. H.R. 4450, as passed by the House, would extend the travel promotion fee though FY2020.

H.R. 938, as passed by the House, and S. 2673, as passed by the Senate, would declare that it is U.S. policy to admit Israel to the VWP when Israel satisfies—and for as long as Israel continues to satisfy—the program's statutory requirements.

Students

The most common nonimmigrant visa for foreign students is the F visa. It is for international students pursuing an education at an "established college, university, seminary, conservatory, academic high school, elementary school, or other academic institution or in an accredited language training program."[72] Both S. 744, as passed by the Senate, and H.R. 2131, as ordered to be reported by the House Judiciary Committee, would make changes to the F visa category. S. 744 would allow aliens on F visas who are seeking a bachelor's or graduate degree to have dual intent; thus, they could seek LPR status while maintaining F status. H.R. 2131 would allow dual intent only for aliens on F visas who are seeking a bachelor's or graduate degree in a STEM field.

S. 744 also would increase the accreditation requirements for schools accepting F students, and would remove the 12 month time limit for foreign students on F visas who are attending public secondary schools.

H.R. 5401, as ordered to be reported by the House Judiciary Committee, would terminate the nonimmigrant status of any Libyan national, or any other foreign national acting on behalf of a Libyan entity, engaging in aviation maintenance, flight operations, or nuclear-related studies or training. In addition, the bill would prohibit these foreign nationals from transferring schools, extending their period of stay, obtaining employment or practical training authorization, reinstating their student status, or changing their nonimmigrant status.

Student and Exchange Visitor Information System (SEVIS)

Congress first mandated a foreign student and exchange visitor tracking system in 1996, and Congress expanded the system's requirements for an electronic tracking system after the September 11, 2001, terrorist attacks.[73] This monitoring system, known as the Student and Exchange Visitor Information System (SEVIS), became operational in 2003, and is administered by ICE's Student and Exchange Visitor Program (SEVP). ICE is developing a new system, known as SEVIS II, in an effort to address limitations in the current SEVIS system. In addition, SEVP certifies schools as being eligible to accept foreign students.

S. 744, as passed by the Senate, and H.R. 2278, as ordered to be reported by the House Judiciary Committee, both contain several provisions related to SEVP and SEVIS.[74] Among other provisions, both S. 744 and H.R. 2278 would change accreditation requirements for academic institutions and flight schools accepting foreign students, and require periodic background checks for those accessing SEVIS. Both bills would make changes to the law to try to accelerate the process of withdrawing a school's certification to prevent problematic institutions from accepting foreign students. Both bills would also increase penalties for fraud related to visa documents committed by the owner or certain employees of SEVP-certified schools, and prohibit individuals convicted of such fraud from holding a position of authority at any school that accepts foreign students. In addition, S. 744 would require DHS to implement a real-time transmission of data from SEVIS to CBP databases. This interoperability would have to be completed within 120 days of enactment or the DHS Secretary would be required to suspend the issuance of foreign student (F and M) visas.

Cultural Exchange Visitors

The J-1 visa is for individuals participating in cultural exchange programs and encompasses a variety of different, often work-related, programs, the largest of which is the summer work/travel program.[75] S. 744 would impose a fee on program sponsors (employers) for each nonimmigrant entering as part of a summer work/travel exchange. In addition, S. 744 would make eligible for a J visa, aliens who are coming to the United States to perform specialized work that requires proficiency in languages spoken in countries with less than 5,000 permanent admissions in the previous year.

PERMANENT ADMISSIONS

Immigrants are persons admitted as legal permanent residents of the United States. Under current law, permanent admissions are subject to a complex set of numerical limits and preference categories that give priority for admission on the basis of family relationships, employment, and geographic diversity of sending countries. These limits include an annual flexible worldwide cap of 675,000 immigrants, plus certain humanitarian admissions. The INA specifies that each year, countries are held to a numerical limit of 7% of the worldwide level of U.S. immigrant admissions, known as per-country limits. The pool of people who are eligible to immigrate to the United States as LPRs each year typically exceeds the worldwide level set by U.S. immigration law, and as a consequence millions of prospective LPRs with approved petitions must wait to receive a numerically limited visa (commonly referred to as the "backlog" or "queue"). The immediate relatives of U.S. citizens are admitted outside of the numerical limits and are the flexible component of the worldwide cap.[76]

S. 744, as passed by the Senate, and H.R. 2131, as ordered to be reported by the House Committee on the Judiciary, would revise the numerical limits on legal permanent immigration and would alter the system that allocates the visas. Both bills would eliminate the per-country ceiling for employment-based preferences, and would increase the per-country ceiling for family-based preferences from 7% to 15%. Both bills would also make substantial changes to the allocation of visas to family-based and employment-based LPRs and would modify rules for investor visas.

Family-Based Immigration

To qualify as a family-based LPR under current law, a foreign national must be the spouse or minor child of a U.S. citizen; the parent, adult child, or sibling of an adult U.S. citizen; or the spouse or unmarried child of a lawful permanent resident. At least 226,000, and no more than 480,000, family preference LPRs are admitted each year within four different preference categories: (1) adult unmarried children of U.S. citizens; (2) spouses, minor children, and adult unmarried children of LPRs; (3) adult married children of U.S. citizens; and (4) siblings of adult U.S. citizens. Foreign nationals who are immediate relatives of U.S. citizens (spouses, minor children, or parents) are not subject to numerical caps and may be admitted in unlimited numbers.[77]

S. 744, as passed by the Senate, includes three sets of provisions that would substantially affect family-based admissions.[78] First, the bill would introduce two "Merit-Based" systems for allocating visas, the second of which would reduce and possibly eliminate the current family-based visa queue of persons with approved immigration petitions, currently estimated at 4.3 million. As discussed more fully below, the Merit-Based Track Two system would allocate LPR visas to family-preference petitioners in the visa queue who had filed before the date of enactment of S. 744. The allocation would occur at a rate of 1/7 of all such pending petitioners per year over the seven years from FY2015 through FY2021. During FY2022-FY2023, visas would be issued to family-preference petitioners filing for up to 18 months after the date of enactment, with half of such petitioners receiving visas in each year (see "Merit-Based Track Two").

In a second set of provisions, S. 744 would alter the number of family-based categories and the applicable numerical limits. It would reclassify spouses and minor unmarried children of LPRs as immediate relatives, making them exempt from family-preference numerical limits. The bill would then reallocate family-preference visas in two stages. In the first stage, during the first 18 months after enactment, family-preference visas would be allocated as follows: (1) adult unmarried children of U.S. citizens would be capped at 20% of the worldwide limit for family-preference immigrants; (2) adult unmarried children of LPRs would be capped at 20% of the worldwide limit, plus unused visas from the first category; (3) adult married children of U.S. citizens would be capped at 20% of the worldwide limit, plus unused visas from the first two categories; and (4) siblings of U.S. citizens would be capped at 40% of the worldwide limit, plus unused visas from the first three categories.

In the second stage, beginning 18 months after enactment, S. 744 would eliminate the fourth preference category for adult siblings of U.S. citizens and would change the third preference category for adult married children. Under the revised system, family-preference visas would be allocated, as follows: (1) adult unmarried children of U.S. citizens could not exceed 35% of the worldwide level; (2) adult unmarried children of LPRs could not exceed 40% of the worldwide level; and (3) adult married children (31 years of age or younger) of U.S. citizens could not exceed 25% of the worldwide level.

A third set of provisions in S. 744 would make nonimmigrant V visas available to all persons with approved petitions pending within a family preference category. Such visas would allow the adult unmarried children of U.S. citizens and LPRs, as well as U.S. citizens' adult married children who are age 31 or younger, to reside in the United States until their visas become available. They would also be granted work authorization during that period.

Employment-Based Immigration

The current employment-based LPR visa system consists of five numerically limited preference categories.[79] To qualify within one of these categories, a foreign national must be: a person of extraordinary or exceptional ability in a specified area; an employee whom a U.S. employer has received approval from the Department of Labor to hire; an investor who will start a business that creates at least 10 new jobs; or someone who meets the narrow definition of the "special immigrant" category.[80] The INA currently allocates 140,000 admissions annually for employment-preference immigrants.

S. 744, as passed by the Senate, would make substantial changes to the employment-based system.[81] Foremost, the bill would exempt from the numerical limits on employment-based LPRs the following:

- derivatives (i.e., accompanying immediate family members) of employment-based LPRs;
- persons of extraordinary ability in the arts, sciences, education, business, or athletics; outstanding professors and researchers; and certain multinational executives and managers (the current first preference employment-based category);
- persons who earned a doctorate degree from an institution of higher education in the United States or an equivalent foreign institution; or persons who earned a graduate degree in a science, technology, engineering, or math (STEM) field from a U.S. institution within the five-year period before the petition filing date and who have a U.S. offer of employment in the related field; and
- foreign national physicians who have completed foreign residence requirements.

In addition to establishing exemptions from numerical limits, the Senate bill would amend existing employment-based preference categories and would change certain procedures for admitting employment-based immigrants. For example, S. 744 would amend the first preference category (described above) to include aliens who are members of the professions holding advanced degrees who have a U.S. job offer (subject to certain requirements), including alien physicians accepted to a U.S. residency or fellowship program, or prospective employees of national security facilities. The second preference category would consist of advanced degree holders and generally would be allocated 40% of the 140,000 employment-based visa total. S. 744 also would change the allocation for the third preference employment-based category (i.e., skilled workers with at least two years training, professionals with baccalaureate degrees, and unskilled workers in occupations in which U.S. workers are in short supply) from 28.6 % to 40% of the worldwide level and would repeal the existing cap of 10,000 on unskilled workers within that 40%.

Rather than shift certain visa categories outside numerical limits as in S. 744, H.R. 2131, as ordered to be reported, would eliminate the family-based fourth preference category for siblings of U.S. citizens (see "Family-Based Immigration") and the diversity visa lottery (see "Diversity Visas"), and would reallocate these visas to increase the total number of employment-based LPR visas to 235,000 per year. The bill would provide up to 55,000 visas for foreign STEM graduates of U.S. universities. Foreign graduates who have a medical, dental or veterinary degree, or who have completed their medical, dental or veterinary residency at a U.S. university, would also be eligible. H.R. 2131 would require the STEM graduates to have completed 85% of their education while being physically present in the United States. Any LPR visas not used by STEM doctorates would be available for those with master's degrees in STEM fields from a U.S. university. In addition, H.R. 2131 would increase to 55,040 each, the number of visas available for immigrants in professions with advanced degrees and persons of exceptional ability, and the number of visas available for skilled workers and professionals with bachelor's degrees. It would not alter the existing cap of 10,000 on unskilled workers.

Investor Visas

The fifth preference category under the current employment-based admissions system is for foreign investors (LPR investors). The basic purpose of the LPR investor visa, commonly referred to as the EB-5 visa, is to benefit the U.S. economy, primarily through employment creation and an influx of foreign capital into the United States. EB-5 visas are designated for individuals wishing to develop a new commercial enterprise in the United States. The INA stipulates that for an investor to qualify for an EB-5 visa, the investor must invest $1 million into the enterprise. The investor receives conditional LPR status, and after two years if USCIS determines that the investor has invested the money, created ten jobs, and the business is still operational, the conditional status is removed. In 1992, the Regional Center Pilot Program was authorized under the EB-5 visa category to provide a coordinated focus for foreign investment toward specific geographic regions. The majority of EB-5 immigrant investors come through the pilot program.

S. 744, as passed by the Senate, and H.R. 2131, as ordered to be reported by the House Judiciary Committee, would make changes to the existing EB-5 program. Both bills would adjust the required amount of capital by the Consumer Price Index for Urban Consumers (CPI-U),[82] and provide procedures for allowing the Secretary of DHS to extend the alien's conditional LPR status if the alien is close to meeting the requirements to have the conditional status removed. Both S. 744 and H.R. 2131 would make the regional center pilot program permanent, and would generally make persons found liable for certain civil, or convicted of certain criminal, offenses ineligible to be involved as an owner, or in management or promotion of, a regional center. Both bills also include procedures for terminating a regional center designation as well as requirements related to ensuring that regional centers comply with securities laws.

In addition to making changes to the existing EB-5 visa category, H.R. 2131 and S. 744 would create new employment-based preference categories for investors, allowing foreign nationals under certain circumstances to receive investment money from qualified investors. Each bill would make a total of about 10,000 new visas available per year under the new categories. The bills contain similar but not identical requirements regarding the amount of money that must be invested and raised, and the number of jobs that must be created within the first three years after investment to have the conditional status removed. S. 744 also includes separate requirements for those who have degrees in a STEM field from a U.S. college or university. In addition, H.R. 2131 would allow E-2 treaty investor visa holders (see "Other Skilled and Professional Workers") to adjust to LPR status under one of the new categories if they meet certain conditions.

Diversity Visas

The purpose of the diversity immigrant visa lottery, as the name suggests, is to encourage legal immigration from countries other than the major sending countries of current immigrants to the United States. The diversity lottery currently makes 50,000 visas available annually to natives of countries that accounted for fewer than 50,000 immigrant admissions in total over the preceding five years.[83]

Some critics of the diversity visa warn that it is vulnerable to fraud and misuse. They argue that the diversity lottery should be eliminated and its visas used for backlog reduction in other visa categories. Supporters of the diversity visa, however, argue that the diversity visa provides "new seed" immigrants for an immigration system weighted disproportionately toward family-based immigrants from a handful of countries. Both S. 744, as passed by the Senate, and H.R. 2131, as ordered to be reported by the House Committee on the Judiciary, would repeal the diversity visa lottery; however, S. 744 would enable those who received diversity visas for FY2013 and FY2014 to be eligible to obtain LPR status.

New Admissions Systems

S. 744, as passed by the Senate, would augment the current preference system of LPR admissions based upon close family relationships and certified employment offers (see preceding "Family-Based Immigration" and "Employment-Based Immigration") with two new pathways. Labeled in the legislation as "Merit-Based" systems, these pathways would enable immigration that is not necessarily dependent on sponsors in the United States and not allocated to achieve country of origin diversity. One system would be designed as a point system to admit aliens based on their employment skills, and the other would be designed to expedite the admission of certain people in the existing visa backlog.

Merit-Based Track One

The proposed Merit-Based Track One visa in Senate-passed S. 744 would admit 120,000 to 250,000 LPRs annually, with the annual flow based upon a sliding formula that would depend on demand for the visa in the previous year. If the average annual unemployment rate in the previous fiscal year was greater than 8.5%, the level would not be increased. Unused visas from past years would be recaptured.

During each of the years FY2015 through FY2017, Track One visas would be made available to foreign nationals who meet existing criteria for the employment-based third preference category for professional, skilled shortage, and unskilled shortage workers. In FY2018 and subsequent years, visas would be allocated as follows:

- 50% would be allocated to Tier 1 based upon factors including education (college plus), employment experience, high-demand occupation, entrepreneurship, relative youth, English language ability, familial relationship to a U.S. citizen, country of origin diversity, and civic engagement.

- 50% would be allocated to Tier 2 based upon factors including employment experience, employment in high-demand occupations that require little to medium preparation (high school diploma or GED), experience as primary caregiver, relative youth, English language ability, familial relationship to a U.S. citizen, country of origin diversity, and civic engagement.

Merit-Based Track Two

S. 744, as passed by the Senate, would create a second Merit System (Track Two) with 4 components. The first component would consist of employment preference petitioners who filed before enactment of S. 744 and whose petitions were pending (i.e., were in the visa queue or backlog) for at least five years on the date of enactment. The second would consist of family-preference petitioners who filed before enactment and whose petitions were pending (i.e., were in the visa queue or backlog) for at least five years. The third component would consist of persons filing third or fourth preference family petitions[84] during the first 18 months after the date of enactment (i.e., before the bill's final changes to the family-preference categories become effective; see "Family-Based Immigration") and whose visas are not issued during the first five years after the bill's date of enactment. The fourth would consist of individuals who have been in a legally present status that allows for employment authorization for 10 years, a category apparently designed to describe unauthorized aliens who would be granted a new registered provisional immigrant status under separate provisions of the bill (see "Legalization of Unauthorized Aliens").

Under S. 744, the first two components of the Merit-Based Track Two system would function as current backlog reduction, as visas would be issued to 1/7 of the petitioners in these two categories, ordered by filing date, during each year from FY2015 through FY2021, regardless of country of origin or other numerical limits. During FY2022-FY2023, Merit-Based Track Two visas would be issued to petitioners filing after the date of enactment under the current family-based third and fourth preference categories, with one half of such filers receiving visas in each of these years (ordered by filing date). These visas would thus accommodate certain family petitioners who no longer would be eligible following the implementation of reforms to the family preference system in S. 744 (see "Family-Based Immigration").

Ten years after enactment of S. 744 (i.e., beginning in FY2024), the Merit-Based Track Two system would become a pathway for individuals granted legal temporary registered provisional immigrant status under the bill to adjust to LPR status (see below). Beginning in FY2029, aliens would be required to have been lawfully present in an "employment authorized status" for 20 years prior to filing for LPR status under Track Two. The bill expressly waives the unlawful presence ground of inadmissibility for Track Two adjustments of status.

LEGALIZATION OF UNAUTHORIZED ALIENS

How to address the unauthorized alien population in the United States is a key and controversial issue in comprehensive immigration reform. There is a fundamental split between those who want to grant legal status to unauthorized aliens in the United States and those who want unauthorized aliens to leave the country.[85] S. 744, as passed by the Senate, proposes to establish legalization programs for certain unauthorized aliens in the United States. The implementation of certain enforcement provisions under Section 3 of S. 744 would serve as pre-conditions for the bill's legalization provisions (see "Border Security Strategy and Metrics").

A general legalization program would initially grant registered provisional immigrant (RPI) status, a new legal temporary status, to unauthorized aliens who have been continuously physically present in the United States since December 31, 2011, and meet other requirements. Dependent spouses and children of these aliens could be classified as RPI dependents if they have maintained continuous physical presence in the United States since December 31, 2012, and meet the other RPI eligibility requirements. RPIs could subsequently apply to adjust to LPR status, subject to specified requirements; there would be a special pathway to LPR status for RPIs who entered the country as children and satisfy criteria under the DREAM Act provisions in S. 744.[86]

RPIs who are not eligible for the DREAM Act pathway would have to adjust to LPR status under the new Merit-Based Track Two system of permanent admissions that S. 744 would separately establish (see "Merit-Based Track Two").

A separate legalization program would grant Blue Card status, another new legal temporary status, to eligible agricultural workers, who could subsequently apply to adjust to LPR status. The general and agricultural legalization programs and the DREAM Act pathway would each be subject to a different set of requirements, which would variously include employment/education, penalty fees, and payment of federal income taxes. The time frames for eligibility for LPR status also vary under the general and agricultural legalization programs and the DREAM Act pathway.[87]

The House has not acted on any legislation to establish a general legalization program for unauthorized aliens. A bill (H.R. 1773) that was ordered to be reported by the House Judiciary Committee, however, would enable certain unauthorized aliens to obtain legal temporary status. H.R. 1773 would establish a new H-2C visa for temporary agricultural workers (see "Agricultural Guest Workers"). The bill includes provisions to permit aliens who were unlawfully present in the United States on April 25, 2013, the day before the bill's date of introduction, to obtain legal temporary status as H-2C agricultural workers. The bill would not provide any special pathway to LPR status for H-2C workers.[88]

NATURALIZATION

A number of bills in the 113th Congress contain provisions amending naturalization, including S. 744, as passed by the Senate, and H.R. 2278, as ordered to be reported by the House Judiciary Committee.[89] Generally, S. 744 would expedite and streamline naturalization, while H.R. 2278 would restrict naturalization. S. 744 would streamline and waive naturalization requirements for certain categories of LPRs, including for certain elderly or physically/mentally disabled applicants, employees of certain national security facilities, and widows of U.S. citizen spouses. In addition, other provisions in S. 744 would: (1) treat U.S. service members who have received combat awards as having satisfied certain naturalization requirements, including good moral character, English/civics knowledge, and honorable service/discharge; (2) develop and expand programs for immigrant integration and naturalization education, outreach, and ceremonies; (3) exempt certain LPRs, who were lawfully present and eligible for work authorization for at least 10 years before becoming LPRs, from the usual residence/physical presence in LPR status required for naturalization;[90] (4) treat admission and periods in registered provisional immigrant status for Dream Act beneficiaries as satisfying admission and periods in LPR status required for naturalization;[91] and (5) amend automatic naturalization for a child born abroad to require physical presence after a lawful admission, instead of residence as an LPR, and to include a person who no longer has legal status nor is physically present in the United States if s/he would have satisfied amended requirements had they been in effect when the person was originally lawfully admitted.

H.R. 2278, among other things, would: (1) bar aliens involved in many terrorism or crime-related activities from satisfying the naturalization requirement for good moral character; (2) clarify that the list of conduct identified in the INA as barring a finding of good moral character is not exhaustive, and that when considering whether an applicant possesses good moral character, immigration authorities may consider that applicant's conduct at any time; (3) bar the naturalization of any alien determined by the Secretary of DHS to have been at any time described in the security-related grounds of deportability or inadmissibility; (4) bar consideration or approval of naturalization applications while proceedings are pending that could result in the applicant's removal, loss of LPR status, or denaturalization; (5) limit judicial review of naturalization delays and denials; (6) purport to authorize the Attorney General to denaturalize persons who have engaged in specified conduct involving terrorism or support for terrorism, the receipt of military training from a terrorist organization, or activities committed with the purpose of overthrowing or opposing the U.S. government through violence or other unlawful means; and (7) strengthen immigration consequences for unlawful procurement of naturalization.[92]

REFUGEE STATUS AND ASYLUM

The United States has long held to the general principle that it will not return a foreign national to a country where his or her life or freedom would be threatened. This principle is embodied in several provisions of the INA, most notably in provisions defining refugees and asylees. Refugees are persons outside their home country who are unable or unwilling to return because of persecution or a well-founded fear of persecution on account of their (1) race, (2) religion, (3) nationality, (4) membership in a particular social group, or (5) political opinion; under certain conditions, refugees may be persons within their home country who are persecuted or have a well-founded fear of persecution on one of these grounds. Refugees are processed and admitted to the United States from abroad.[93]

Foreign nationals may claim asylum in the United States if they demonstrate a well-founded fear that if returned home, they will be persecuted based upon one of the five grounds enumerated above. They may apply for asylum affirmatively with USCIS after arrival into the country, or they may seek asylum defensively before an immigration judge during removal proceedings.[94]

S. 744, as passed by the Senate, would increase the flexibility of the INA asylum and refugee provisions in several ways. For example, S. 744 would repeal a current provision that requires asylum claims to be filed within one year of an alien's arrival in the United States, and would provide for the reconsideration of certain asylum claims that were denied because of the failure to file within one year. Under certain circumstances, a U.S. asylum officer would be authorized to grant asylum to an alien found to have a credible fear of persecution based on an interview during expedited removal rather than referring the alien to an immigration judge. The bill also would authorize the spouse or child of a refugee or asylee who is admitted to the United States to bring his or her own accompanying child in the same status.

S. 744 would establish requirements for overseas refugee adjudications, including the right to legal counsel (not at government expense), a written record of the decision, and administrative review of a denial. Other refugee-related provisions would authorize the President, based on a recommendation by DOS, to designate certain groups of aliens on the basis of humanitarian concerns or national interest, and thereby facilitate the admission of group members as refugees. In addition, a new category of "stateless persons" would be defined, and such persons would be permitted to apply for conditional lawful status under certain conditions, and to adjust to LPR status after one year under the employment-based preference category for special immigrants.

At the same time, S. 744 includes provisions that would tighten refugee and asylum laws for national security purposes. Specifically, an alien granted refugee status or asylum who returns to his or her country of nationality or habitual residence would have that refugee or asylee status terminated unless the DHS Secretary determines that the alien returned for good cause, or another exception applies. S. 744 also would expand law enforcement and national security checks during the refugee and asylum application process. (See "Inadmissibility, Deportability, and Relief from Removal" for a related discussion.)

Lautenberg Amendment

Special legislative provisions facilitate relief for certain refugee groups. The "Lautenberg amendment," first enacted in 1989, required the Attorney

General (now the Secretary of DHS) to designate categories of former Soviet and Indochinese nationals for whom less evidence would be needed to prove refugee status, and provided for adjustment to LPR status for certain former Soviet and Indochinese nationals denied refugee status. P.L. 108-199 amended the Lautenberg amendment to add a new provision, known as the "Specter amendment," to direct the Attorney General to establish categories of Iranian religious minorities who may qualify for refugee status under the Lautenberg amendment's reduced evidentiary standard. The Consolidated and Further Continuing Appropriations Act, 2013 (P.L. 113-6) extended the Lautenberg amendment through FY2013. The amendment subsequently lapsed but was re-enacted as part of P.L. 113-76 for the remainder of FY2014. Language to extend the amendment through FY2015 is included in House-reported and Senate-reported FY2015 Department of State, Foreign Operations, and Related Programs Appropriations bills (H.R. 5013, S. 2499).

IMMIGRATION PROVISIONS OF THE VIOLENCE AGAINST WOMEN ACT

Foreign national spouses of U.S. citizens and LPRs can acquire legal status through the family-based immigration provisions of the INA. In general, they must be sponsored by their U.S. citizen or LPR spouses and meet the requirements for LPR status.[95] The INA also includes provisions to assist foreign national victims of domestic abuse and allow them to self-petition for LPR status independently of their U.S. citizen or LPR relatives.[96] These provisions, which were initially enacted in the Immigration Act of 1990 (P.L. 101-649) and the Violence Against Women Act (VAWA) of 1994 (P.L. 103-322, Title IV), have been periodically reauthorized. The 2000 reauthorization (VAWA 2000), part of the larger Victims of Trafficking and Violence Protection Act (TVPA, P.L. 106-386), created the nonimmigrant U visa for foreign national victims of certain crimes—including domestic abuse—who assist law enforcement to investigate and prosecute such crimes. Successful petitioners for such a visa are classified as U nonimmigrants for up to four years. Program authorizations in VAWA expired in 2011. Efforts to reauthorize the VAWA programs in the 113th Congress culminated in the enactment of Violence Against Women Reauthorization Act of 2013 (P.L. 113-4).

Among its immigration-related provisions, P.L. 113-4 includes "stalking" in the definition of criminal activity covered under the U visa. It extends VAWA coverage to "derivative" children who are included in their parents' petitions and whose parents die during the petition process. It exempts VAWA self-petitioners, U visa petitioners, and battered foreign nationals from being classified as inadmissible for LPR status if their financial circumstances raise concerns over their becoming potential public charges. It protects U visa petitioners under age 21 and derivative children of adult U visa petitioners from aging out of eligibility if they reach age 21 after filing a U visa petition. The law also includes a provision that allows DHS to share VAWA petition information with other government agencies for national security purposes.

P.L. 113-4 includes additional protections for foreign nationals who intend to marry U.S. citizens and LPRs. These provisions require increased disclosure about U.S. citizen and LPR sponsors and more stringent restrictions for international marriage brokers.

The law requires DHS to provide foreign nationals with information about inconsistent self-disclosures by sponsors regarding past domestic abuse and to conduct more extensive background checks on each U.S. citizen who petitions on behalf of an alien fiancé/fiancée to provide the latter with additional information about potentially abusive relationships. It prohibits international marriage brokers from marketing information about foreign nationals under age 18 and requires more extensive record-keeping of age-related documentation. It expands federal criminal penalties for specified marriage broker and other VAWA violations.

S. 744, as passed by the Senate, also includes several VAWA-related provisions. It would expand the number of U visas from 10,000 to 18,000 annually. It would grant aging-out protection, deferred status eligibility (to allow spouses and children of nonimmigrant visa holders to receive independent immigration status), and work authorization eligibility to any derivative child on a VAWA petition. It would provide financial relief to VAWA petitioners by requiring that DHS grant them work authorization no later than six months following the petition filing date. It would allow VAWA applicants to adjust to LPR status without being subject to the family-based immigration numerical limits.

Finally, S. 744 would permit battered immigrants access to public housing.

TRAFFICKING VICTIMS PROTECTION ACT

It is a crime to engage in trafficking in persons (TIP) for the purposes of commercial exploitation. TIP involves violations of labor, public health, and human rights standards. The 2000 TVPA created a new visa category for victims of severe forms of trafficking (T visa).[97] The 2000 act and subsequent reauthorizations also created several grant programs to aid trafficking victims and to train law enforcement to combat TIP. P.L. 113-4 modifies some of the grant programs under the TVPA,[98] expands reporting requirements, creates new criminal penalties for trafficking offenses, modifies the criteria for T visas, and reauthorizes appropriations for FY2014 through FY2017.[99]

P.L. 113-4 makes it a criminal offense to knowingly destroy, or for a period of more than 48 hours, conceal, remove, confiscate, or possess, another person's passport or immigration or personal identification documents in the course of committing or attempting to commit the offense of fraud in foreign labor contracting or alien smuggling, and allows for civil remedies for personal injuries caused during the commission of most criminal trafficking offenses.

P.L. 113-4 makes the adult or minor children of a beneficiary of derivative T status eligible for T status if it is determined that such a person faces a present danger of retaliation as a result of the trafficking victim's cooperation with law enforcement. In addition, P.L. 113-4 amends the grant program for state and local law enforcement's anti-trafficking programs that focus on U.S. citizen victims,[100] so that the grants can also be used for anti-trafficking programs for noncitizen victims.

Several other bills in the 113th Congress would further amend the TVPA.[101] H.R. 3610, as passed by the House, would amend the TVPA to require that, beginning in FY2017, the Secretary of the Department of Health and Human Services (HHS) award grants for a national communication system to help victims of severe forms of trafficking communicate with service providers. The bill would also require the Attorney General to collect and tabulate data on mandatory restitution orders (the TVPA requires the court to order restitution—to be paid by the defendant to the victim—for any crime of peonage, slavery, or trafficking in persons). H.R. 3530, as passed by the House, would authorize the Attorney General to award grants to an eligible entity[102] to develop, improve, or expand domestic child human trafficking deterrence programs designed to aid victims while investigating and prosecuting the trafficking offenses. H.R. 5135, as passed by the House, would require the Interagency Task Force to Monitor and Combat Trafficking to produce a report on preventing child trafficking, and would clarify that services for trafficking victims can include housing.

Unaccompanied Alien Children

The William Wilberforce Trafficking Victims Protection Reauthorization Act of 2008 (TVPRA, P.L. 110-457) contained provisions creating procedures for screening unaccompanied alien children (UAC) from contiguous countries, and for the care, custody, processing, and repatriation of all UAC.[103] P.L. 113-4 amends and expands the TVPRA provisions dealing with the care and custody of unaccompanied minors. The act specifies that the DHS Secretary should consider placing in the least restrictive setting any unaccompanied alien child who turns 18 while in HHS custody.[104] The act also requires the DHS Secretary to create a pilot program at a limited number of immigration detention sites to provide independent child advocates for child trafficking victims and other vulnerable unaccompanied alien children. In addition, P.L. 113-4 specifies that children who receive U status and are in the custody of HHS are eligible for programs and services to the same extent as refugees, and that the federal government will reimburse states for foster care provided to these children. As mentioned under "Border Security," there has been a large increase in the number of UAC apprehended along the Southwest border in recent years, which has led Congress to evaluate the procedures and processes related to UAC. Division B of H.R. 5230, as passed by the House, would amend the TVPRA and the INA to change the procedures for screening and processing unaccompanied alien children who arrive at the U.S. border from certain countries.[105] H.R. 5230 also would require the HHS Office of Refugee Resettlement (ORR) to perform a biometric criminal history check as part of the suitability assessment to place an unaccompanied child with a family member or sponsor in the United States and would bar the placement of such children with sex offenders or human traffickers.[106]

OTHER ISSUES AND LEGISLATION

U.S. Territories

Most inhabited U.S. territories, including Puerto Rico, Guam, the Virgin Islands, and the Commonwealth of the Northern Mariana Islands (CNMI), are defined by the INA as included in the definition of "United States" for the purpose of federal immigration laws. The notable exception is American Samoa (including Swain's Island), which has its own *sui generis* immigration system and whose native residents are non-citizen U.S. nationals under the INA. American Samoans who move to the United States, as this term is defined in the INA, are eligible for expedited naturalization. In the 113th Congress, several bills would establish specific accommodations for the circumstances and immigration needs of the CNMI.

Title VII of P.L. 110-229 made the INA applicable to the CNMI, a U.S. territory in the Pacific. Previously, in accordance with an agreement known as the Covenant[107] that sets forth the relationship between the CNMI and the United States, the territory had not been subject to U.S. immigration law. Among other provisions, P.L. 110-229 established a transition period for implementing the INA in the CNMI that began on November 28, 2009, and is scheduled to end on December 31, 2014. This law aimed, in particular, to provide federal regulation and oversight of the admission of foreign workers to the territory, including by establishing a CNMI-only transitional worker visa. It also provided for a CNMI-only investor visa for persons who previously had investor permits under the territorial system. Aliens who were not eligible for the transitional foreign worker or investor visas or other visas under federal immigration laws were able to remain in the CNMI on entry permits issued under the former territorial immigration laws until the earlier of the original permit expiration date or November 28, 2011.[108]

S. 1237, as passed by the Senate, and H.R. 4296, as ordered to be reported by the House Natural Resources Committee, would extend the transition period for implementing the INA in the CNMI until December 31, 2019. S. 744, as passed by the Senate, would resolve the status of certain long-term foreign residents of the CNMI who were unable to otherwise acquire LPR status under the federal system.[109] It would authorize admission of these various long-term foreign residents, subject to certain requirements, as immigrants to the CNMI only, and provide a path for most of these CNMI-only residents to adjust later to regular LPR status.

Iraqi Special Immigrant Visa Program

The Iraqi special immigrant visa program, which was established by Section 1244 of P.L. 110-181 and subsequently amended by P.L. 110-242, makes Iraqi nationals eligible for special immigrant status if they: were employed by or on behalf of the U.S. government in Iraq for not less than one year during a specified period; provided documented valuable service to the U.S. government; and have experienced "an ongoing serious threat as a consequence of the alien's employment by the United States government." This program had been capped at 5,000 principal aliens (excluding spouses and children) for each of fiscal years 2008 through 2012 and allowed for unused visa numbers to be carried forward from one year to the next through FY2013. P.L. 113- 42 amended the numerical limitations provisions to extend the Iraqi special immigrant visa program and provide additional visas. It set the total number of principal aliens who could be provided special immigrant status under the program for the first three months of FY2014 at the sum of the number of aliens with pending applications on September 30, 2013, plus 2,000. Initial applications for new cases (subject to the 2,000 limit) had to be submitted to the DOS Chief of Mission in Iraq by December 31, 2013. The National Defense Authorization Act for Fiscal Year, 2014 (P.L. 113-66) rewrites the extension language in P.L. 113-42 to provide for the issuance of no more than 2,500 visas to principal applicants after January 1, 2014, and to extend the application deadline to September 30, 2014.[110]

Afghan Special Immigrant Visa Program

P.L. 111-8 established a special immigrant program for Afghans modeled on the Iraqi program (see "Iraqi Special Immigrant Visa Program"). Under the program, Afghan nationals are eligible for special immigrant status if they were employed by or on behalf of the U.S. government in Afghanistan for not less than one year during a specified period; provided documented valuable service to the U.S. government; and have experienced "an ongoing serious threat as a consequence of the alien's employment by the United States government." The Afghan special immigrant program was originally capped at 1,500 principal aliens annually for FY2009 through FY2013, with a provision to carry forward any unused numbers from one fiscal year to the next.

In the 113th Congress, P.L. 113-76 amended the Afghan program's numerical limitation provisions to provide for the granting of special immigrant visas to up to 3,000 principal aliens for FY2014 and to provide for the carry forward and use of any unused balance through the end of FY2015. This law required that principal aliens file an application with the Chief of Mission in Afghanistan by September 30, 2014. P.L. 113-160 further amends the numerical limitations provisions under the Afghan program to provide that an additional 1,000 principal aliens may be granted special immigrant status by December 31, 2014. The new language requires that principal aliens apply to the Chief of Mission no later than the same December 31, 2014, date.[111]

House-passed H.R. 4435 and Senate-reported S. 2410 would make additional changes to the Afghan special immigrant program. H.R. 4435 would replace the numerical limitations language enacted in P.L. 113-160 with new language to provide up to 1,075 Afghan special immigrant visas for FY2015 (in addition to any unused numbers from FY2014). Under this bill, principal aliens would need to apply to the Chief of Mission by September 30, 2015. S. 2410, as reported by the Senate Armed Services Committee, would provide that for each of FY2014 and FY2015, up to 4,000 principal aliens could be granted special immigrant visas, with any unused balance carried forward and available through December 31, 2016. Principal aliens would need to apply to the Chief of Mission by December 31, 2015. S. 2410 also would expand eligibility for the Afghan special immigrant program. In addition to aliens employed in Afghanistan by or on behalf of the U.S. government, the eligible population would include aliens employed in Afghanistan by or on behalf of an organization closely associated with the U.S. mission in Afghanistan that has received U.S. government funding through an official contract, award, grant, or cooperative agreement.

Other Legislation Receiving Action

International Adoptions

The Accuracy for Adoptees Act (P.L. 113-74) amends Section 320 of the INA regarding the citizenship of adopted foreign-born children by requiring that all federal documents issued or amended, including a certificate of citizenship, reflect the child's name and date of birth, as shown on state vital records following the adoption or readoption in that state.

ICE Public Advocate

In 2012, ICE created the Public Advocate Office "to assist individuals and representatives who have concerns about ICE operations and policies in the field."[112] The office was created in response to critiques that the agency was unresponsive to the complaints of those who were detained or investigated. However, some contend that the program is not productive and is not a proper use of ICE resources.[113] P.L. 113-6, the FY2013 Consolidated and Further Continuing Appropriations Act, stated that no funds under the act could be used to fund the position of Public Advocate within ICE. Nonetheless, some argue that the position of Public Advocate was simply renamed Deputy Assistant Director of Custody Programs and Community Outreach, and that the functions of the disbanded Public Advocate Office are currently being performed under the umbrella of "community outreach."[114] H.R. 3732, as ordered to be reported by the House Judiciary Committee, would prohibit federal funds from being used to provide funding for the following positions within ICE: Public Advocate; Deputy Assistant Director of Custody Programs and Community Outreach; or any other position with similar functions.

End Notes

[1] For a summary of the major provisions of S. 744, see CRS Report R43099, *Comprehensive Immigration Reform in the 113th Congress: Short Summary of Senate-Passed S. 744*, by Ruth Ellen Wasem; for a fuller discussion of the major provisions of S. 744, see CRS Report R43097, *Comprehensive Immigration Reform in the 113th Congress: Major Provisions in Senate-Passed S. 744*, by Ruth Ellen Wasem.

[2] For further discussion of issues related to unaccompanied children, see CRS Report R43599, *Unaccompanied Alien Children: An Overview*; CRS Report R43734, *Unaccompanied Alien Children: Demographics in Brief;* CRS Report R43623, *Unaccompanied Alien Children—Legal Issues: Answers to Frequently Asked Questions*; CRS Report R43664, *Asylum Policies for Unaccompanied Children Compared with Expedited Removal Policies for Unauthorized Adults: In Brief;* CRS Report R43702, *Unaccompanied Children from Central America: Foreign Policy Considerations*.

[3] DHS appropriations, for the most part, are not covered here. See CRS Report R43147, *Department of Homeland Security: FY2014 Appropriations*.

[4] For data on Southwest border apprehensions, see CRS Report R43523, *Apprehensions of Unauthorized Migrants along the Southwest Border: Fact Sheet*; for a discussion of unaccompanied child arrivals, see CRS Report R43599, *Unaccompanied Alien Children: An Overview*.

[5] For further discussion of border security strategies, see CRS Report R42969, *Border Security: Understanding Threats at U.S. Borders*; for further discussion of border security metrics, see CRS Report R42138, *Border Security: Immigration Enforcement Between Ports of Entry*.

[6] See CRS Report R43097, *Comprehensive Immigration Reform in the 113th Congress: Major Provisions in Senate-Passed S. 744*.

[7] These triggers are described in S. 744 §3(c). For a fuller discussion, see Ibid.

[8] S. 744 §3(a)(3). The "effectiveness rate" would be statutorily defined in a similar manner to the way the term is currently used internally by USBP: the sum of alien apprehensions and turn-backs divided by total estimated illegal entries. S. 744 §3(a)(4). Also see U.S. Government Accountability Office, *Border Patrol: Key Elements of Strategic Plan Not Yet in Place to Inform Border Security Status and Resource Needs*, GAO-13-25, December 2012.

[9] H.R. 1417 §3(o)(8).

[10] See CRS Report R42138, *Border Security: Immigration Enforcement Between Ports of Entry*.

[11] For a fuller discussion see CRS Report R43097, *Comprehensive Immigration Reform in the 113th Congress: Major Provisions in Senate-Passed S. 744.*

[12] Direct spending does not require additional legislative action to go into effect, in contrast with authorizations for discretionary spending, which require separate appropriations bills to go into effect.

[13] U.S. Congress, Senate Committee on Homeland Security and Governmental Affairs, *Border Patrol Agent Pay Reform Act*, report to accompany S. 1691, 113th Congress, 2d sess., S.Rept. 113-248, p. 1.

[14] Biometric data include fingerprints and digital photographs, and may be used to confirm an individual's identity against previously recorded biometric data (i.e., by matching fingerprints); biographic data include names, birthdates, and other identifying information and can be connected to an individual's case history and immigration records, but cannot confirm the identity of arriving and departing passengers. In general, visitors traveling by air or sea are required to provide biometric data at ports of entry, and carriers provide DHS with biographic data (based on passenger lists) upon their exit. For further discussion of the entry-exit system, see CRS Report R43356, *Border Security: Immigration Inspections at Ports of Entry.*

[15] S. 744 §3303(c).

[16] See CRS Report R42346, *Federal Land Ownership: Overview and Data*; also see U.S. Government Accountability Office, *Border Security: Additional Actions Needed to Better Ensure a Coordinated Federal Response to Illegal Activity on Federal Lands*, GAO-11-177, November 2010, p. 15.

[17] See for example, U.S. Congress, House Committee on Natural Resources, Subcommittee on National Parks, Forests, and Public Lands, *The Border: Are Environmental Laws and Regulation Impeding Security and Harming the Environment?*, 112th Cong., 1st sess., April 15, 2011.

[18] See, among other laws, the National Environmental Policy Act of 1969 (42 U.S.C. §§4321 *et seq.*), the Endangered Species Act of 1973 (16 U.S.C. §§1531 *et seq.*), and the National Historic Preservation Act (16 U.S.C. §§470 *et seq.*).

[19] See archived CRS Report RL33659, *Border Security: Barriers Along the U.S. International Border.*

[20] See CRS Legal Sidebar WSLG536, Proposed Waiver Authority for Border Construction Is Not New, But Is It Improved?

[21] U.S. Department of Homeland Security, "Determination Pursuant to Section 102 of the Illegal Immigration Reform and Immigrant Responsibility Act of 1996, as Amended," 73 *Federal Register* 19077-19078, April 8, 2008.

[22] Act of June 27, 1952, ch. 477; 66 Stat. 163; codified as amended at 8 U.S.C. §1101 et seq. The INA is the basis of current immigration law.

[23] For more extensive discussion of modifications made by the bills, including changes not discussed here, see CRS Report R43097, *Comprehensive Immigration Reform in the 113th Congress: Major Provisions in Senate-Passed S. 744*, and CRS Report R43192, *Immigration Enforcement: Major Provisions in H.R. 2278, the Strengthen and Fortify Enforcement Act (SAFE Act).*

[24] For background on existing criminal offenses, see CRS Legal Sidebar CRS Report WSLG563, *An Overview of Immigration-Related Crimes.*

[25] INA §275

[26] INA §276

[27] See CRS Report R41104, *Immigration Visa Issuances and Grounds for Exclusion: Policy and Trends*, and CRS Report RL32480, *Immigration Consequences of Criminal Activity*.

[28] INA §101(a)(43) provides a list of crimes deemed to be aggravated felonies for immigration purposes, a list that Congress has repeatedly expanded over the years to cover additional crimes. The definition is not limited to offenses punishable as felonies (i.e., punishable by at least a year and a day imprisonment); certain misdemeanors are also defined as aggravated felonies for INA purposes. See generally CRS Legal Sidebar CRS Report WSLG454, *Will Immigration Reform Legislation Revisit the Definition of "Aggravated Felony"?* and archived CRS Report RL32480, *Immigration Consequences of Criminal Activity*.

[29] The grounds of inadmissibility generally apply to aliens who have not been lawfully admitted into the United States, including (1) aliens outside the United States who seek to obtain a visa or admission at a port of entry; (2) aliens within the United States who seek to adjust their status to that of an LPR; and (3) aliens who entered the United States unlawfully. The grounds for deportability, in contrast, apply to aliens who were lawfully admitted into the United States.

[30] For discussion of detention policy and practices, see CRS Report RL32369, *Immigration-Related Detention*.

[31] Several courts have interpreted provisions of the INA requiring the mandatory detention of certain categories of aliens as having implicit temporal limitations, in order to avoid resolving constitutional questions that would be raised if the INA were construed to permit the prolonged or indefinite detention of aliens. See CRS Legal Sidebar CRS Report WSLG524, *How "Mandatory" Is the Mandatory Detention of Certain Aliens in Removal Proceedings?*

[32] S. 744 §3715.

[33] Gary Mead, Executive Associate Director, ICE, et al., Applicability of Prosecutorial Discretion Memoranda to Certain Family Relationships, Oct. 5, 2012, reproduced in 89 *Interpreter Releases* 1966-67 (Oct. 15, 2012).

[34] Under the DACA initiative, certain individuals who were brought to the United States as children and meet other criteria can be considered for temporary administrative relief from removal for two years, subject to renewal. See CRS Report R43747, *Deferred Action for Childhood Arrivals (DACA): Frequently Asked Questions*.

[35] For further discussion of prosecutorial discretion in immigration enforcement, see CRS Report R42924, *Prosecutorial Discretion in Immigration Enforcement: Legal Issues*.

[36] See, generally, CRS Report R41423, *Authority of State and Local Police to Enforce Federal Immigration Law*; CRS Report R41991, *State and Local Restrictions on Employing Unauthorized Aliens*; and CRS Report R42719, *Arizona v. United States: A Limited Role for States in Immigration Enforcement*.

[37] Arizona v. United States, 132 S. Ct. 2492, __ U.S. __ (2012). For further discussion, see CRS Report R42719, *Arizona v. United States: A Limited Role for States in Immigration Enforcement*.

[38] INA §287(g) authorizes the Secretary of DHS to enter written agreements that enable specially trained state or local officers to perform specific functions relative to the investigation, apprehension, or detention of aliens, during a predetermined time frame and under federal supervision. For further discussion, see CRS Report R42057, *Interior Immigration Enforcement: Programs Targeting Criminal Aliens*.

[39] While E-Verify is primarily a voluntary program, there are some mandatory participants. See CRS Report R40446, *Electronic Employment Eligibility Verification*.

[40] For additional information on E-Verify, see Ibid.

[41] See, for example, S. 202, H.R. 478, and H.R. 502, as introduced in the 113th Congress.

[42] H.R. 1772 §12.

[43] USCIS currently makes such a photo tool available through the E-Verify system for certain identity documents. Under S. 744, DHS would be required to develop another mechanism for documents not covered by the photo tool.

[44] These regulations would have to be published not later than one year after the date of enactment.

[45] DHS could require an employer that is found to have engaged in a pattern or practice of violations of U.S. immigration laws to verify its current employees through the EVS.

[46] For further discussion of the compliance and penalty provisions in S. 744, see CRS Report R43097, *Comprehensive Immigration Reform in the 113th Congress: Major Provisions in Senate-Passed S. 744.*

[47] See CRS Report R41104, *Immigration Visa Issuances and Grounds for Exclusion: Policy and Trends.*

[48] For example, USCIS approves immigrant petitions, ICE operates the Visa Security Program in selected U.S. embassies abroad, and CBP inspects all people who enter the United States.

[49] H.R. 2278 §§405, 402. H.R. 2278 would also eliminate language in INA §222(f) providing that the sharing of visa or permit-related information with foreign governments shall be "on the basis of reciprocity."

[50] H.R. 2278 §403.

[51] This new authority for DHS would supplement INA §221(i), which provides that after a visa has been issued, the consular officer and the Secretary of State have discretion to revoke the visa at any time. For further discussion, see CRS Report R43192, *Immigration Enforcement: Major Provisions in H.R. 2278, the Strengthen and Fortify Enforcement Act (SAFE Act).*

[52] U.S. Government Accountability Office, *Border Security: DHS's Visa Security Program Needs to Improve Performance Evaluation and Better Address Visa Risk Worldwide*, GAO-11-315, March 31, 2011.

[53] Lawful permanent residents, also known as immigrants and green card holders, are noncitizens who are legally authorized to reside permanently in the United States.

[54] See CRS Report RL31381, *U.S. Immigration Policy on Temporary Admissions.*

[55] For a fuller discussion of H-1B visas, see CRS Report R42530, *Immigration of Foreign Nationals with Science, Technology, Engineering, and Mathematics (STEM) Degrees.*

[56] For a fuller discussion, see CRS Report RL33977, *Immigration of Foreign Workers: Labor Market Tests and Protections.*

[57] E-1 visas are for treaty traders and the E-2 are for treaty investors. For more on the E category, see CRS Report RL33844, *Foreign Investor Visas: Policies and Issues.*

[58] Free trade agreements are not considered treaties of commerce and navigation.

[59] For further discussion of proposed changes in S. 744 to these and other nonimmigrant categories, see CRS Report R43097, *Comprehensive Immigration Reform in the 113th Congress: Major Provisions in Senate-Passed S. 744.*

[60] See CRS Report R42434, *Immigration of Temporary Lower-Skilled Workers: Current Policy and Related Issues.*

[61] See CRS Report R43161, *Agricultural Guest Workers: Legislative Activity in the 113th Congress.*

[62] See CRS Report R43097, *Comprehensive Immigration Reform in the 113th Congress: Major Provisions in Senate-Passed S. 744.*

[63] The length of stay may be extended for an additional 180 days.

[64] For more on this category, see CRS Report R43097, *Comprehensive Immigration Reform in the 113th Congress: Major Provisions in Senate-Passed S. 744.*

[65] As of October 2014, there are 38 countries that are eligible to participate in the VWP. For more on the VWP, see CRS Report RL32221, *Visa Waiver Program.*

[66] The nonimmigrant refusal rate is the number of people from the country who were refused a B tourist visa in the previous year and who could not overcome the denial, divided by the total number of people from the country who applied for a B visa in the previous year.

[67] The nonimmigrant overstay rate is the number of people from the country on B visas who did not leave the United States when their term of admittance ended during the previous year, divided by the total number of people from that country who were admitted on B visas and were supposed to leave the United States during the previous year.

[68] For more details on the provisions in S. 744 regarding the VWP, see CRS Report R43097, *Comprehensive Immigration Reform in the 113th Congress: Major Provisions in Senate-Passed S. 744.*

[69] For additional information, see Ibid. and CRS Report RL32221, *Visa Waiver Program.*

[70] The VWP provisions in S. 744 are almost identical to those in H.R. 1354.

[71] BrandUSA was established by the Travel Promotion Act of 2009 (P.L. 111-145). For more on Brand USA, see CRS Report R43463, *U.S. Travel and Tourism: Industry Trends and Policy Issues for Congress.* The total ESTA fee is $14, which includes $4 to cover the costs of administering ESTA and $10 for the travel promotion fee.

[72] INA §101(a)(15)(F).

[73] Illegal Immigration Reform and Immigrant Responsibility Act of 1996 (IIRIRA, P.L. 104-208), USA Patriot Act of 2001 (P.L. 107-56), and Enhanced Border Security and Visa Reform Act of 2002 (P.L. 107-173). For more on the history of SEVIS, see archived CRS Report RL32188, *Monitoring Foreign Students in the United States: The Student and Exchange Visitor Information System (SEVIS).*

[74] For more on these provisions, see CRS Report R43097, *Comprehensive Immigration Reform in the 113th Congress: Major Provisions in Senate-Passed S. 744.*

[75] The J visa category includes professors and research scholars, students, foreign medical graduates, teachers, interns, summer workers, camp counselors, and au pairs who are participating in an approved exchange visitor program. For additional information on the summer work/travel program, see CRS Report R42434, *Immigration of Temporary Lower-Skilled Workers: Current Policy and Related Issues.*

[76] See CRS Report R42866, *Permanent Legal Immigration to the United States: Policy Overview.*

[77] For information on the current family-based preference categories and visa allocations, see CRS Report R43145, *U.S. Family-Based Immigration Policy.*

[78] See CRS Report R43097, *Comprehensive Immigration Reform in the 113th Congress: Major Provisions in Senate-Passed S. 744.*

[79] For a list of current preference categories, see CRS Report R42866, *Permanent Legal Immigration to the United States: Policy Overview.*

[80] Special immigrants include ministers of religion, religious workers, and certain employees of the U.S. government abroad, among other groups.

[81] For a more detailed discussion of these changes, see CRS Report R43097, *Comprehensive Immigration Reform in the 113th Congress: Major Provisions in Senate-Passed S. 744.*

[82] The CPI-U is a measure that examines the weighted average of prices of selected consumer goods and services, such as transportation, food, and medical care.

[83] See CRS Report R41747, *Diversity Immigrant Visa Lottery Issues.*

[84] The existing third preference family-based category is for adult married children of U.S. citizens; the fourth preference family-based category is for siblings of adult U.S. citizens.

[85] Among those supportive of granting legal status to unauthorized aliens, there are further splits between those who support granting legal status to the majority of unauthorized aliens and those who favor legalizing only selected groups.

[86] The DREAM Act, which stands for the Development, Relief, and Education for Alien Minors Act, refers broadly to legislation introduced regularly in Congress to enable certain unauthorized aliens in the United States to obtain legal permanent resident status. For information on the DREAM Act provisions in S. 744, see CRS Report R43097, *Comprehensive Immigration Reform in the 113th Congress: Major Provisions in Senate-Passed S. 744.*

[87] See Ibid.

[88] See CRS Report R43161, *Agricultural Guest Workers: Legislative Activity in the 113th Congress.*

[89] Other bills include, for example, H.R. 932, S. 296, and S. 645.

[90] This provision would cover eligible aliens granted registered provisional immigrant status under S. 744 and would enable them to naturalize after three years in LPR status, subject to applicable requirements. See CRS Report R43097, *Comprehensive Immigration Reform in the 113th Congress: Major Provisions in Senate-Passed S. 744.*

[91] However, such DREAM Act beneficiaries could not apply for naturalization while in RPI status unless applying for military-service-based naturalization pursuant to INA §§328 and 329. See Ibid.

[92] *See* CRS Report R43192, *Immigration Enforcement: Major Provisions in H.R. 2278, the Strengthen and Fortify Enforcement Act (SAFE Act).*

[93] See CRS Report RL31269, *Refugee Admissions and Resettlement Policy.*

[94] See CRS Report R41753, *Asylum and "Credible Fear" Issues in U.S. Immigration Policy* . For a discussion of asylum policies applicable to unaccompanied children, see CRS Report R43664, *Asylum Policies for Unaccompanied Children Compared with Expedited Removal Policies for Unauthorized Adults: In Brief.*

[95] INA §204.

[96] For more information, see CRS Report R42477, *Immigration Provisions of the Violence Against Women Act (VAWA).*

[97] To be eligible for T status, with certain exceptions regarding the age and the mental health of the victim, the victim is required to cooperate with law enforcement.

[98] These include grant programs for victims' services and law enforcement anti-trafficking activities.

[99] For background information and a full discussion of the trafficking-related provisions in P.L. 113-4, see CRS Report RL34317, *Trafficking in Persons: U.S. Policy and Issues for Congress.*

[100] This grant program was created in P.L. 109-164, §204.

[101] For a discussion of human trafficking legislation, see CRS Report R43555, *Domestic Human Trafficking Legislation in the 113th Congress.*

[102] An eligible entity would be a state or unit of local government that meets specified criteria.

[103] UAC are defined in statute as children who lack lawful immigration status in the United States, are under the age of 18, and are without a parent or legal guardian in the United States or for whom no parent or legal guardian in the United States is available to provide care and physical custody (6 U.S.C. §279(g)(2)). For more on the issue of unaccompanied alien children, see CRS Report R43599, *Unaccompanied Alien Children: An Overview*, and

CRS Report R43623, *Unaccompanied Alien Children—Legal Issues: Answers to Frequently Asked Questions*.

[104] Unaccompanied alien children are placed in HHS custody. Unaccompanied alien children who turn 18 while in HHS custody are transferred to ICE custody.

[105] Additionally, House-passed H.R. 5230 includes provisions on assistance to Central American countries for repatriation and reintegration programs. The bill would condition funding for such programs on a country's cooperation in efforts to reduce illegal migration to the United States.

[106] Unaccompanied alien children who are apprehended by CBP or ICE and who either are ineligible for, or do not accept, voluntarily return are placed in ORR custody. ORR arranges to house the child in one of its shelters or in a foster care situation, or most commonly, to reunite the child with a family member. See CRS Report R43599, *Unaccompanied Alien Children: An Overview*.

[107] The Covenant To Establish a Commonwealth of the Northern Mariana Islands In Political Union with the United States of America, codified at 48 U.S.C. §1801 note.

[108] In the fall of 2011, USCIS announced that certain groups of permit holders would be eligible for parole beyond the final permit expiration date, including (1) long-term foreign residents of the CNMI, namely immediate relatives of U.S. citizens and certain persons born in the CNMI who did not receive U.S. citizenship (also their spouses and unmarried children under 21 years old); (2) caregivers of U.S. citizens or LPRs with critical medical or special needs; (3) transitional workers' dependents turning 18 within one year; and (4) beneficiaries of certain pending nonimmigrant worker petitions. Parole would be granted on a case-by-case, discretionary basis and would permit recipients to stay lawfully in the CNMI. Parole is a form of immigration relief that does not constitute formal admission into the United States but permits an alien to come to and/or stay in the United States temporarily for humanitarian or public interest reasons. USCIS guidelines for parole benefitting these groups are available at http://www.uscis.gov/portal/site/uscis/ menuitem.eb1d4c2a3e5b9ac89243c6a7543f6d1a/?vgnextoid=4d3314dd2b635210VgnVCM100000082ca60aRCRD& vgnextchannel=4d3314dd2b635210VgnVCM100000082ca60aRCRD.

[109] For background information on these residents, see archived CRS Report R42036, *Immigration Legislation and Issues in the 112th Congress*.

[110] See CRS Report R43725, *Iraqi and Afghan Special Immigrant Visa Programs*.

[111] See Ibid.

[112] Department of Homeland Security, *Teleconference Recap: A Conversation with U.S. Immigration and Customs Enforcement (ICE) Public Advocate*, Washington , DC, March 28, 2012, http://www.dhs.gov/teleconference-recapconversation-us-immigration

[113] See, for example, Stephen Dinan, "Senate Democrats Join Push to Cut Obama's Illegal Immigrant Advocate," *The Washington Times*, March 12, 2013, http://www.washington times.com/news/2013/mar/12/senate-spending-billincludes-elimination-of-new-i/?page=all.

[114] See §2 of H.R. 3732.

In: Immigration Policy Proposals ...
Editor: Kimberly D. Parsons

ISBN: 978-1-63482-344-9

Chapter 3

THE PRESIDENT'S IMMIGRATION ACCOUNTABILITY EXECUTIVE ACTION OF NOVEMBER 20, 2014: OVERVIEW AND ISSUES*

William A. Kandel, Jerome P. Bjelopera, Andorra Bruno and Alison Siskin

SUMMARY

On November 20, 2014, President Obama announced his Immigration Accountability Executive Action which revises some U.S. immigration policies and initiates several programs, including a revised border security policy for the Southwest border; deferred action programs for some unauthorized aliens; revised interior enforcement priorities; changes to aid the entry of skilled workers; the promotion of immigrant integration and naturalization; and several other initiatives the President indicated would improve the U.S. immigration system. The most controversial among these provisions will grant deferred action to as many as 5 million unauthorized aliens.

---

* This is an edited, reformatted and augmented version of a Congressional Research Service publication R43852, prepared for Members and Committees of Congress dated January 8, 2015.

The President announced the executive actions through ten Department of Homeland Security (DHS) memoranda, two White House memoranda, and three Department of Labor (DOL) fact sheets. Together, they comprise the following initiatives:

- ***Border Security*****:** forming three new task forces as part of DHS's Southern Border and Approaches Campaign Strategy that integrates efforts not only *within* DHS's Customs and Border Protection (CBP) but also among other DHS agencies, such as Immigration and Customs Enforcement (ICE), U.S. Citizenship and Immigration Services (USCIS), and the U.S. Coast Guard;
- ***Interior Enforcement and Removals*****:** revising priorities for immigration enforcement and detention; ending the Secure Communities program and replacing it with the Priority Enforcement Program (PEP), collecting and disseminating improved metrics on removals, and reforming the employment structure for ICE Enforcement and Removal Office (ERO) agents;
- ***Expanded Deferred Action for Childhood Arrivals (DACA)*****:** increasing the population eligible for the DACA program by expanding the eligibility criteria, and extending the duration of DACA and its related work authorization from two to three years;
- ***Deferred Action for Parents of Americans and Lawful Permanent Residents (DAPA)*****:** allowing parents of U.S. citizens and lawful permanent residents (LPRs) to request deferred action and employment authorization if they meet residency and other criteria and pass required background checks;
- ***Parole Rules*****:** revising conditions under which eligible family members of military personnel, persons traveling abroad, and certain entrepreneurs may receive parole;
- ***Provisional Unlawful Presence Waivers*****:** expanding the use of provisional unlawful presence waivers beyond spouses and minor children of U.S. citizens to also include the spouses and minor children of LPRs as well as the adult children of U.S. citizens, and clarifying the "extreme hardship" standard that must be met to obtain this waiver;
- ***High Skilled Workers*****:** ensuring that all statutorily available LPR visas are fully utilized, reviewing the labor certification program and its regulations to strengthen its integrity and responsiveness to workforce changes, providing foreign workers with greater flexibility

to change jobs, expanding the use of national interest waivers to retain selected highly qualified workers, expanding opportunities for students to gain on-the-job training through administrative rule changes, and clarifying the meaning of "specialized knowledge" to ensure U.S. workers are not being unfairly displaced;

- ***Immigrant Integration and Naturalization*****:** initiating an inter-agency task force to identify and promote both immigrant integration "best practices" within states and localities as well as facilitating steps that can be taken administratively within and among federal agencies, and encouraging eligible LPRs to naturalize through additional payment options and possible partial fee waivers;
- ***Immigrant Visa System*****:** providing recommendations to streamline, modernize, and improve immigrant and nonimmigrant visa processing;
- ***Labor Protection*****:** creating an inter-agency working group to promote effective and consistent enforcement of federal labor, employment, and immigration laws to protect all workers regardless of legal status; and
- ***Crime Victims*****:** expanding the DOL Wage and Hour Division's role in supporting foreign national victims of human trafficking and other select crimes.

According to the President, the actions were taken in response to the absence of legislation addressing major problems within the immigration system. The President has stated that his actions are temporary, and that his successor can rescind them. Those opposed to the executive actions argue they were taken largely for political purposes. They contend that once granted, such temporary measures would be difficult to revoke. Separately, a debate has arisen as to whether the President has the legal authority to take such actions, with the Administration and others arguing the President's actions fall within his authority, and many in Congress arguing the President has overstepped it. That debate and its attendant legal questions are beyond the scope of this report.

Because the President announced his executive actions relatively recently, little guidance is available to clarify policies and answer questions related to the revisions and initiatives they include. The two deferred action programs, both of which require petitioners to submit fees, are the only initiatives in the executive action supported by independent fee-supported funding. The rest rely largely on changes in rules and regulations and on the coordination and marshaling of existing administrative resources. As the Administration proceeds to implement the executive actions, some in Congress have vowed to halt some or all of them.

INTRODUCTION

On November 20, 2014, President Obama announced his Immigration Accountability Executive Action which revises some U.S. immigration policies and initiates several programs, including a revised border security policy for the Southwest border; deferred action programs for some unauthorized aliens; revised interior enforcement priorities; changes to aid the entry of skilled workers; the promotion of immigrant integration and naturalization; and several other initiatives the President indicated would improve the U.S. immigration system. The most controversial among these provisions will grant deferred action to as many as 5 million unauthorized aliens.[1] The President announced the executive action through ten Department of Homeland Security (DHS) memoranda, two White House memoranda, and three Department of Labor (DOL) fact sheets.

According to the President, the actions were taken in response to the absence of legislation addressing major problems within the immigration system. The President has stated that his actions are temporary, and that his successor can rescind them. Those opposed to the executive actions argue they were taken largely for political purposes. They contend that once granted, such temporary measures would be difficult to revoke. Separately, a debate has arisen as to whether the President has the legal authority to take such actions, with the Administration and others arguing the President's actions fall within his authority, and many in Congress arguing the President has overstepped it.[2] That debate and its attendant legal questions are beyond the scope of this report. As the Administration proceeds to implement the executive actions, some in Congress have vowed to halt some or all of them.

Overview of Major U.S. Immigration Policy Issues

Policy makers and immigration observers widely agree that the U.S. immigration system is "broken," but they disagree on measures to fix it. Underlying these different views are broader and more fundamental debates about how many temporary and permanent immigrants should be admitted into the United States, how those immigrants should be selected for admission (e.g., needed skills, relationship to U.S. residents), and the funding levels and appropriate mix of immigration enforcement measures, among other issues.[3]

Long-standing immigration-related challenges include: an estimated population of over 10 million unauthorized individuals, a large portion of whom have lived in the country for over a decade and have U.S. citizen and lawful permanent resident (LPR) children;[4] increasing competition among more advanced nations for the "best and brightest" workers, including U.S. educated science, technology, engineering, and mathematics (STEM) graduates;[5] a queue of 4.4 million individuals whose petitions for lawful permanent resident (LPR) status have been approved and who must wait, in some cases decades, for a numerically limited visa to immigrate;[6] and ongoing border security and interior enforcement challenges.[7]

Broad Elements of Immigration Reform

For several years, some Members of Congress have favored "comprehensive immigration reform" (CIR), a label that commonly refers to omnibus legislation that includes increased border security and immigration enforcement, expanded employment eligibility verification, revision of nonimmigrant visas and legal permanent immigration, and legalization for some unauthorized aliens residing in the country. The omnibus legislative approach contrasts with incremental revisions of the Immigration and Nationality Act (INA) and other immigration laws that would address some but not all of these elements, and with sequential reforms that would tackle border security and interior enforcement provisions prior to revising legal immigration or enacting legalization pathways for the unauthorized population residing in the United States.

In 2013, the Senate passed the Border Security, Economic Opportunity, and Immigration Modernization Act (S. 744), a comprehensive immigration reform bill. S. 744 contained provisions that, among other things, would have increased border security and interior enforcement, expanded employment eligibility verification and worksite enforcement, offered a conditional path to legal status for many unauthorized aliens, reformed permanent immigrant and temporary nonimmigrant visas, and revised humanitarian admissions. The House took a different approach to immigration reform. Rather than consider a single comprehensive bill, the House acted on separate bills that, among other provisions, would have increased border security and interior enforcement, expanded employment eligibility verification and worksite enforcement, and substantially revised nonimmigrant and immigrant visas.[8]

Summary of the President's Executive Action

The President's "Immigration Accountability Executive Action," announced on November 20, 2014, includes initiatives covering the following policy areas:

- border security;
- interior enforcement and removals;
- Deferred Action for Childhood Arrivals (DACA);
- Deferred Action for Parents of Americans and Lawful Permanent Residents (DAPA);
- parole;
- provisional unlawful presence waivers;
- high-skilled foreign workers;
- immigrant integration and naturalization;
- immigrant visa system;
- labor protection; and
- crime victims.

This report reviews each component of the President's executive action based on currently available information. The report is broken out by broad policy areas. Each section begins with a discussion of the context of existing policy, describes the related executive action, and summarizes how the action addresses current immigration policy challenges.

BORDER SECURITY

Security along U.S. borders has been an ongoing subject of congressional interest since the 1970s, when illegal immigration emerged as a serious national problem. The terrorist attacks of September 11, 2001 (9/11) spurred concerns about border security, a core part of DHS's effort to control unauthorized migration. The United States Border Patrol (USBP, Border

Patrol) spearheads this effort as the lead agency along most of the borders. The USBP focuses on the regions between ports of entry (POEs).[9]

In addition to Border Patrol agents, other law enforcement personnel work in U.S. border regions. These include Customs and Border Protection (CBP) officers at POEs; Immigration and Customs Enforcement (ICE) agents; U.S. Coast Guard (USCG) personnel; additional federal law enforcement officers from agencies such as the Drug Enforcement Administration, U.S. Marshals Service, and Department of Agriculture; state and local police; and on occasion, the National Guard. Complementing this array of personnel are CBP's land-based surveillance assets,[10] air and marine surveillance assets,[11] and fencing and physical infrastructure.[12]

USBP has experienced large-scale growth since 2004, and DHS Secretary Johnson and the Obama Administration have argued that the Southwest border is more secure than ever.[13] Yet, some Members of Congress and others have called on the Administration to do more to secure the border. Border security has been a recurrent theme in Congress's debate about comprehensive immigration reform since 2005, and some Members have argued that Congress should not consider additional immigration reforms until the border is more secure.[14]

USBP is responsible for enforcing U.S. immigration law and other federal laws along the border and for preventing all unlawful entries into the United States, including entries of terrorists, unauthorized aliens, weapons of mass destruction, illicit narcotics, and other contraband. In discharging its duties, USBP patrols roughly 7,500 miles of U.S. international borders with Mexico and Canada and the coastal waters around Florida and Puerto Rico.

Along the border, USBP's staffing has grown from 9,511 in FY2004 to 18,611 in FY2013, with a slight dip to 18,127 in FY2014 (Figure 1). At the same time, apprehensions at the Southwest border have declined with an uptick in recent years partly due to a rise in the number of unaccompanied children crossing illegally. It is unclear how the expansion in USBP personnel has influenced unlawful migration, but the Obama Administration and DHS Secretary Johnson have touted these two numbers as indicative of improved security along the Southwest border.[15]

In recent years, CBP and USBP have developed border security plans. In May 2012, CBP released the most recent iteration, the "2012-2016 Border Patrol Strategic Plan." It shifts attention from resource acquisition and deployment to the strategic allocation of resources by "focusing enhanced capabilities against the highest threats and rapidly responding along the border."[16] From an operational perspective, this plan emphasizes the collection and analysis of information about evolving border threats; integration of Border Patrol and CBP planning across different border sectors and among the full range of federal, state, local, tribal, and international organizations involved in border security; and rapid Border Patrol response to specific border threats.[17]

Coordinating Border Security

In one project to enhance the coordination of complex border security and inspection efforts, CBP developed the Arizona Joint Field Command (JFC). The JFC emerged in 2011 as "an organizational realignment" bringing together the Border Patrol with CBP's other key components,[18] "under a unified command structure to integrate CBP's border security, commercial enforcement, and trade facilitation missions to more effectively meet the unique challenges faced in the Arizona area of operations."[19] The JFC includes more than 6,700 CBP employees and covers the entire state of Arizona and parts of California.

FY2004-FY2014

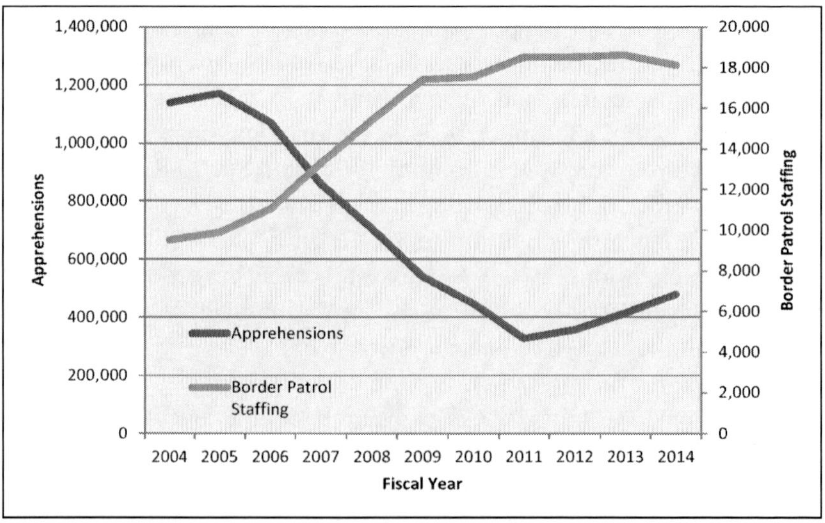

Source: Jeh Charles Johnson, DHS Secretary, "Border Security in the 21st Century," slides from presentation delivered at the Center for Strategic and International Studies, Washington, DC, October 9, 2014.

Figure 1. Apprehensions and Border Patrol Staffing along the Southwest Border.

DHS has announced coordination measures that appear to go much further than the JFC. Secretary Johnson first revealed the development of such border-security plans in May 2014. In written congressional testimony he describes a "Southern Border and Approaches Campaign" planning effort devised to create

> a strategic framework to further enhance security of our Southern border. Plan development will be guided by specific outcomes and quantifiable targets for border security, approved by me, and will address improved information sharing, continued enhancement and integration of sensors, and unified command and control structures as appropriate. The overall planning effort will also include a subset of campaign plans focused on addressing challenges within specific geographic areas.[20]

Discussion

On November 20, 2014, DHS Secretary Johnson expanded on the campaign by "commissioning" three Joint Task Forces.[21] Unlike the Arizona JFC, which brings together elements *within* CBP, the three Joint Task Forces will bring together personnel from CBP as well as *other* DHS agencies—the U.S. Coast Guard, Immigration and Customs Enforcement, and U.S. Citizenship and Immigration Services (USCIS). The Joint Task Forces will also "integrate capabilities of the remaining [DHS] components as needed." According to Secretary Johnson, "two of these task forces will be geographically based and one will be functionally focused." Joint Task Force East will cover "the Southern maritime border and approaches." Joint Task Force West will have responsibility for the southern land border and the West Coast, while an entity dubbed Joint Task Force Investigations "will focus on investigations in support of the geographic Task Forces." The memo lays out broad missions and objectives and sets a 90 day timeframe to "realign personnel and stand up headquarters capabilities within each Joint Task Force."

Thus far, more details about the Joint Task Forces are scarce, and several key questions loom:

- Will DHS alter its command and control structures—as well as those of its component agencies—to accommodate these new bodies?

- What authority will each Joint Task Force leader[22] have over Task Force personnel, immediate priorities, and budgets? Will such authority supersede the authority of component leadership in DHS?
- What metrics will be used to assess the effectiveness of the Joint Task Forces?
- How will jurisdictional disputes between Joint Task Forces and issues related to competing mission priorities be settled?

Enforcement Priorities, Secure Communities, and Pay Reform

Since its enactment in 1952, the Immigration and Nationality Act has given the Attorney General and more recently the DHS Secretary discretion to exercise the power to remove foreign nationals. Since at least 1975, a series of policy memorandums published by the former Immigration and Naturalization Service (INS) and DHS has provided guidance to immigration officers who institute removal proceedings against an alien. The guidance noted which categories of foreign nationals to prioritize for removal (i.e., prosecutorial discretion).[23]

ICE Enforcement and Removal Operations (ERO) is chiefly responsible for locating removable aliens, managing custody of aliens undergoing removal procedures, and ensuring that aliens directed to depart from the United States do so (either by witnessing their removals or by physically removing the aliens). In addition, certain other DHS personnel may initiate a removal process against an alien.[24]

On November 20, 2014, the DHS Secretary announced new department-wide policies for enforcement priorities and the apprehension, detention, and removal of aliens.[25] This guidance is effective on January 5, 2015. In addition, Secretary Johnson announced a review and actions to overhaul the pay scale for immigration officers in ERO.[26]

Enforcement Priorities

Secretary Johnson wrote in the November 20, 2014 memorandum on enforcement priorities:

> Due to limited resources, DHS and its components cannot respond to all immigration violations or remove all persons illegally in the United States. As is true of virtually every other law enforcement agency, DHS must exercise prosecutorial discretion in the enforcement of the law. And, in the exercise of that discretion, DHS can and should develop smart enforcement priorities, and ensure that use of its limited resources is devoted to the pursuit of those priorities.[27]

The memorandum states that prosecutorial discretion should apply to initiating or suspending a removal proceeding as well as other enforcement decisions, such as deciding who to stop, question, arrest and detain; whether to continue to pursue a removal case; and whether to grant deferred action, parole, or a stay of removal. While DHS may exercise prosecutorial discretion at any stage of an enforcement proceeding, the policy states it is preferable to do so as early as possible to conserve government resources.

The memorandum lays out the following enforcement priorities:

- *(Highest) Priority 1: threats to national security, border security, and public safety*
    - aliens engaged in or suspected of terrorism or espionage, or who otherwise pose a threat to national security;
    - aliens apprehended at the border or ports of entry while attempting to unlawfully enter the United States;
    - aliens convicted of an offense that involves participating in a criminal street gang,[28] or aliens who are 16 years or older who intentionally participated in an organized criminal gang to further illegal activity of the gang; and
    - aliens convicted of felonies.[29]
- *Priority 2: misdemeanants and new immigration violators*
    - aliens convicted of three or more misdemeanors[30] or a "significant misdemeanor;"[31]
    - aliens who are unlawfully present and were not physically present before January 1, 2014; and
    - aliens who have significantly abused the "visa or visa waiver programs" (i.e., terms of admittance).
- *Priority 3: aliens issued final orders of removal after December 31, 2013.*

According to the memorandum, unless certain circumstances are met, aliens described in *Priority 1* must be prioritized for removal, those in Priority 2 should be removed, and those in *Priority 3* should generally be removed.[32]

The President's executive action issued on November 20, 2014, revises enforcement priorities and rescinds and supersedes related policies issued in 2011 and 2012 by then-ICE Director John Morton.[33] The previous priority levels were (1) aliens who pose a danger to national security or a risk to public safety; (2) recent entrants; and (3) aliens with final orders of removal (i.e., fugitives or absconders) or who otherwise obstruct immigration controls. The most substantive change in enforcement priorities between the newly issued policy and policies from earlier years[34] is that an alien who was issued a final order of removal prior to 2014 is no longer an enforcement priority, provided he or she is neither a criminal nor a national security concern.[35] Other changes include increasing the priority level of aliens apprehended at or between ports of entry while attempting to illegally enter the country, and providing more specificity on the types of misdemeanor offenses that make an alien a focus for removal.

Detention Priorities

As with the previous Morton policy memorandum on detention and removal priorities,[36] the November 20, 2014, memorandum on enforcement priorities specifies that as a general rule, detention resources should be used to support enforcement priorities noted above or for aliens subject to mandatory detention under the law.[37] In keeping with earlier policy, the memorandum also states that, absent extraordinary circumstances or the statutory requirement of mandatory detention, ICE should not detain aliens who are

- known to be suffering from serious physical or mental illness;
- disabled, elderly, pregnant, or nursing;
- primary caretakers of children or infirm persons; or
- not in the public interest to detain.

Removal Statistics

ICE and the Office of Immigration Statistics (OIS) both report removal statistics, but immigration observers have raised questions about their accuracy.[38] In addition, removal statistics are used to evaluate DHS's adherence to stated policies on enforcement priorities.[39] Through the executive action, DHS Secretary Johnson directs OIS, with the cooperation of CBP, ICE, and USCIS, to create the capability to collect and maintain data reflecting the numbers of those apprehended, removed, returned, or otherwise repatriated by any component of DHS. He further directs that these statistics be made publically available on an annual basis.

Secure Communities/Interoperability

Secure Communities was the original name given to an information sharing program that uses biometric data to screen for removable aliens as people are being booked into jails. The program began in late 2008 in about a dozen jurisdictions and since FY2013 has been operational in all state and local law enforcement jurisdictions in the country. As early as 2011, DHS began referring to this program as *interoperability* between local law enforcement, the Federal Bureau of Investigation (FBI), and DHS.[40]

Secure Communities/interoperability is not an enforcement unit. When law enforcement agencies book (take custody of) someone and submit the person's fingerprints to the FBI for criminal background checks,[41] the fingerprints are also automatically checked against DHS's Automated Biometric Identification System (IDENT) database.[42] If the person is matched to an immigration record in IDENT, ICE is notified and determines whether any action is necessary or appropriate based on the agency's enforcement priorities.[43] Aliens identified for removal are placed in removal proceedings by ICE agents, typically from the Criminal Alien program (CAP).[44]

As part of the President's executive action, Secretary Johnson directs ICE to discontinue Secure Communities.[45] However, the data interoperability between DOJ and DHS created under the name Secure Communities is not being discontinued. Instead, the program is being renamed and enforcement priorities changed for those identified as possibly removable aliens through the interoperability process. Consistent with the policy memorandum on enforcement priorities, the policy memorandum on Secure Communities specifies that ICE should only seek a transfer for an alien in state or local custody if he or she has been convicted of a *Priority 1* offense or of multiple or significant misdemeanors. Under the revised priorities, unless aliens pose a demonstrable risk to national security, enforcement actions will only be taken against those convicted of specifically enumerated crimes. The new program will be called the Priority Enforcement Program (PEP).

The Secure Communities memorandum also addresses the issue of "immigration detainers." These are documents in which ICE advises law enforcement agencies of its interest in individuals whom these agencies are detaining, and to take actions (such as holding the alien temporarily) to facilitate their removal.[46] The increased use of immigration detainers under Secure Communities has raised legal questions regarding their use.[47] Under the revised policy, ICE will replace requests for detention with requests for notification (i.e., that state or local law enforcement notify ICE of an alien's pending release from custody). Under special circumstances, a detention request may be issued if the person is subject to a final order of removal or if sufficient probable cause exists to find the person removable.

Some contend that the Secure Communities program has led to unfair treatment of selected individuals (e.g., a person is arrested rather than just given a warning or ticket because of his or her perceived immigration status) as well as some improper arrests and unlawful detention (e.g., a person is arrested on a false change because he or she is perceived to be unlawfully present).[48] In the Secure Communities memorandum of November 20, 2014, the DHS Secretary directs the Office of Civil Rights and Civil Liberties to develop and implement a plan to monitor state and local law enforcement agencies participating in the transfer of foreign nationals to ICE.

Personnel Reform

As part of the President's executive action, DHS also announced a recalibration of the workforce and pay structure for ICE Enforcement and Removal Operations (ERO) personnel."[49] The related memorandum directs ERO and the DHS Office of the Chief Human Capital Officer to review the job series and premium pay coverage for ERO officers and determine any changes that may be required. The Administration will then pursue and prioritize regulations and legislation necessary to achieve the desired changes. According to the Administration, ERO's enforcement strategy and initiatives have shifted toward investigations, identification, location, arrest, prosecution, and removal of criminal aliens and other aliens who pose risks to national security. However, ERO's personnel structure lags behind other law enforcement agencies and other components of ICE, harming morale and presenting management challenges.[50] Some observers contend that personnel issues related to pay structure have existed for years at ERO, and that the reforms within the President's executive actions were timed for political purposes.[51]

Discussion

Since 2002, DHS has made concerted efforts to locate and remove absconders.[52] The President's executive action of November 20, 2014 no longer makes such aliens enforcement priorities if they were issued final orders of removal prior to 2014 and are neither criminals nor national security concerns. At the start of FY2014, ICE reported a backlog of 469,151 fugitive aliens who had not been apprehended.[53] The Administration stated it is undertaking this policy to allow DHS to focus its limited resources on higher enforcement priorities. It is not known, however, how many fugitive aliens would qualify for the President's deferred action initiatives, but some overlap between the two programs can be expected. Time will be required to measure the impact of the new enforcement priorities on the types of aliens who are located and removed.

In addition, until implemented it remains unclear exactly what the effect of the new PEP program will be, compared to the former and in some ways comparable Secure Communities program it replaced. The enforcement priorities memorandum of November 20, 2014, suggests that ICE will issue fewer detainers with state and local law enforcement, focusing only on higher priority cases. It is also unclear how well the new requests for notification will effectuate the transfer of aliens to ICE custody, given that not all jurisdictions currently accept ICE requests for detention.

Deferred Action, Parole, and Provisional Inadmissibility Waivers

How to address the unauthorized alien[54] population in the United States has arguably been the most divisive issue in recent discussions about immigration reform. Proposals to enable unauthorized aliens to become U.S. lawful permanent residents (LPRs) have been key flash points in the congressional debate. Various legalization proposals have been introduced in recent Congresses, but none have been enacted. One key difference among these proposals has been their scope. Some bills have been targeted at particular segments of the unauthorized population. For example, legislation known as the Development, Relief, and Education for Alien Minors (DREAM) Act has proposed to enable certain unauthorized aliens who arrived in the United States as children to obtain LPR status through a two-stage process.[55] Other more controversial measures, such as the major Senate immigration reform bill considered in the 113th Congress,[56] have aimed to provide LPR status more broadly.

While only legislative action can bestow legal immigration status, the Obama Administration has used other mechanisms to enable unauthorized aliens to remain in the United States. The Administration has also taken steps to address the impact of provisions in the Immigration and Nationality Act (INA) that make aliens who have been unlawfully present in the United States for more than 180 days and then depart, inadmissible to the country for a specified period of time. These provisions are known as the 3- and 10-year bars. Through a recent set of executive actions, the Obama Administration is providing eligibility for two forms of temporary immigration relief—deferred action and parole—for certain segments of the unauthorized population, as well as expanding the availability of certain types of waivers of the unlawful presence grounds of inadmissibility in the INA.[57]

Deferred Action

DHS defines deferred action as "a discretionary determination to defer removal action of an individual as an act of prosecutorial discretion."[58] In 2012, in the absence of congressional action on DREAM Act legislation, DHS issued a memorandum announcing that certain unauthorized individuals who were brought to the United States as children and meet other criteria would be considered on a case-by-case basis for deferred action for two years, subject to renewal.[59] The eligibility criteria established for this initiative, known as deferred action for childhood arrivals, or DACA, were similar to those for relief in DREAM Act bills. Among the DACA criteria were (1) being under age 16 at time of entry into the United States; (2) residing continuously in the United States since June 15, 2007; and (3) being below age 31 on June 15, 2012. The DACA initiative is administered by DHS's U.S. Citizenship and Immigration Services (USCIS). Aliens apply for employment authorization at the same time that they submit their applications for consideration of DACA.[60]

On November 20, 2014, DHS Secretary Johnson announced an expansion of the original DACA initiative and the establishment of another DACA-like process to exercise prosecutorial discretion for another subgroup of unauthorized aliens in the United States.[61]

Expansion of Eligibility for DACA

The 2014 DHS memorandum on prosecutorial discretion directs USCIS to make specified changes to the DACA initiative that expand the pool of potential beneficiaries, as follows:

- elimination of the "below age 31 on June 15, 2012" requirement;
- advancement of the required starting date of continuous residence from June 15, 2007, to January 1, 2010; and
- extension of the initial grant and renewal periods for DACA and accompanying employment authorization from two to three years.

In the memorandum, DHS directs USCIS to begin accepting applications under the expanded DACA parameters in 90 days.

Establishment of the New Deferred Action Process

In the memorandum, the DHS Secretary further directs USCIS to establish a DACA-like process for exercising prosecutorial discretion toward another group of unauthorized individuals—parents of U.S. citizens or LPRs—who meet specified criteria. In addition to not having a lawful immigration status on November 20, 2014, a potential beneficiary must:

- be the parent of a U.S. citizen or LPR;
- have resided continuously in the United States since before January 1, 2010;
- be physically present in the United States on November 20, 2014, and at the time of making a request for consideration of deferred action with USCIS;
- not be an enforcement priority; and
- not present any other factors that make the grant of deferred action inappropriate.

The memorandum specifies that, as under DACA, applicants will apply for employment authorization at the same time that they submit their applications for consideration of deferred action. Grants of deferred action and accompanying work authorization under this process will be valid for a three-year period. In the memorandum, the DHS Secretary directs USCIS to begin accepting applications under the new deferred action process within 180 days.

Deferred action is also addressed in another DHS memorandum where the DHS Secretary directs USCIS to consider granting deferred action to unauthorized family members of U.S. military service members and veterans who are not eligible for parole-in-place (see "Parole").[62]

Parole

The INA authorizes the DHS Secretary to "parole into the United States temporarily under such conditions as he may prescribe only on a case-by-case basis for urgent humanitarian reasons or significant public benefit any alien applying for admission into the United States."[63] Parole does not constitute formal admission to the United States; an individual granted parole is still considered an applicant for admission. Although parole is used most often to allow an alien who is outside the United States to enter the country, it also has been granted to unauthorized aliens who are physically present in the United States but who have never been lawfully admitted.[64] Parole granted to those present in the United States is known as *parole-in-place*. Another procedure, advance parole, may be authorized by USCIS to enable an alien in the United States to travel abroad and, upon return, be considered for parole.

Expansion of Use of Parole-in-Place for Military Families

Ongoing DHS policy makes certain family members of U.S military service members and veterans eligible for parole-in-place. Covered family members are spouses, children, and parents of active duty members—and former members—of the U.S. Armed Forces and the Selected Reserve of the Ready Reserve.[65] In his November 20, 2014 memorandum, the DHS Secretary reports that the Department of Defense (DOD) has requested that DHS expand the application of its military parole-in-place policy to cover family members of U.S. citizens and LPRs who seek to enlist in the U.S. Armed Forces.[66] In the memorandum, the Secretary directs USCIS to issue new policies on the use of parole-in-place for certain spouses, children, and parents of U.S. citizens and LPRs seeking to enlist.

Advance Parole

The November 20, 2014, DHS memorandum *Directive to Provide Consistency Regarding Advance Parole* addresses a Board of Immigration Appeals (BIA)[67] decision concerning advance parole and one of the grounds of inadmissibility in the INA related to unlawful presence.[68] In the *Matter of Arrabally*, the BIA decided that "individuals who travel abroad after a grant of advance parole do not effectuate a 'departure . . . from the United States' within the meaning of [INA] section 212(a)(9)(B)(i)."[69] Under INA §212(a)(9)(B)(i)(1), an alien who has been unlawfully present in the United States for more than 180 days but less than one year, voluntarily departs, and seeks admission within three years is inadmissible (3-year bar); and under INA §212(a)(9)(B)(i) (2), an alien who has been unlawfully present in the United States for one year or more and seeks admission within 10 years of such alien's departure or removal date is inadmissible (10-year bar). If, in accordance with the *Arabally* decision, travel on advance parole does not constitute a departure, then the 3- and 10-year bars on admissibility would not be triggered in such cases. In the DHS memorandum, the DHS Secretary provides notice that he has asked the DHS General Counsel to issue legal guidance clarifying that "in all cases when an individual physically leaves the United States pursuant to a grant of advance parole, that individual shall not have made a 'departure' within the meaning of section 212(a)(9)(B)(i) of the INA."

Provisional Unlawful Presence Waivers

The INA provides for specified family members of U.S. citizens or LPRs and specified categories of workers to be admitted to the United States for permanent residence as LPRs. The process of becoming an LPR through either the family-based or employment-based route has multiple steps.[70] In most cases, the sponsoring family member or employer must file an immigrant visa petition on behalf of the alien with USCIS.[71] Among the general requirements for obtaining a visa or gaining lawful admission to the United States is that an individual must be admissible to the country. In other words, the individual cannot be inadmissible under the enumerated grounds of inadmissibility in the INA (see "Advance Parole"). Some grounds of inadmissibility are subject to exceptions and waivers.

Unauthorized aliens in the United States with approved immigrant visa petitions may face difficulties in obtaining LPR status. The process of becoming an LPR from within the United States is known as *adjustment of status*. The main adjustment of status provision in the INA[72] applies to aliens who have been inspected and admitted, or paroled, into the United States or who qualify for classification under the Violence Against Women Act (VAWA) and who meet other specified requirements. These requirements include that (1) the alien is the beneficiary of an approved immigrant visa petition; (2) an immigrant visa is immediately available;[73] and (3) the alien is admissible to the United States. Except for VAWA cases, unauthorized aliens who entered the United States without inspection are ineligible to adjust to LPR status under the main INA adjustment of status provision. Unauthorized aliens who initially were admitted or paroled into the country are generally ineligible to adjust status unless they qualify for an exception.[74]

The alternative to adjusting status in the United States is for the alien to travel to his or her home country to apply for a visa at a U.S. embassy or consulate once a visa number becomes immediately available. If a visa is issued, the alien can use it to gain lawful admission to the United States as an LPR. If, however, an unauthorized alien returns home to apply for a visa, the Department of State (DOS) consular officer who is considering the visa application may find that the alien is inadmissible to the United States for 3 or 10 years based on the alien's prior unlawful presence in the United States, and thereby ineligible for a visa (see "Advance Parole").

A prospective immigrant who is found to be ineligible for a visa by DOS based on his or her prior unlawful presence may be eligible for a waiver. Under INA §212(a)(9)(B)(v), DHS has discretionary authority to grant an alien a waiver if the alien is the spouse or son or daughter of a U.S. citizen or LPR, and it is established that refusal of admission to the alien would result in extreme hardship to the citizen or LPR spouse or parent. Until recently, an alien had to wait until he or she received an ineligibility finding from DOS during the overseas immigrant visa process before applying for a waiver, if eligible.

In 2013, USCIS issued a new rule that made changes to the unlawful presence waiver application process for certain spouses and minor children of U.S. citizens by establishing a provisional unlawful presence waiver. Under the rule, a beneficiary of an approved immigrant visa petition can apply for and receive a provisional waiver of the unlawful presence ground of inadmissibility while still in the United States, if the alien meets all the applicable requirements, including demonstrating that a U.S. citizen spouse or parent would experience extreme hardship if the alien were denied admission to the United States. A recipient of a provisional waiver can then depart the

United States to attend an immigrant visa interview with a DOS consular officer abroad. If the consular officer determines that the applicant, given the approved waiver, is admissible to the United States and eligible for a visa, the officer may issue the immigrant visa, which the individual can present at a port-of-entry to gain lawful admission to the United States.

Expansion of Eligibility for Provisional Unlawful Presence Waivers

As noted, DHS has statutory discretionary authority to grant an unlawful presence waiver to an alien who is the spouse or son or daughter of a U.S. citizen or LPR. Under current regulations, however, eligibility for a provisional waiver is limited to spouses and minor children of U.S. citizens. As part of the President's executive action, the DHS Secretary directs USCIS to expand eligibility for provisional unlawful presence waivers to all statutorily eligible groups for whom an immigrant visa is immediately available.[75] The additional classes to be covered are adult children of U.S. citizens; and spouses, minor children, and adult children of LPRs.

Clarification of Extreme Hardship Standard

In order to receive an unlawful presence waiver under INA §212(a)(9)(B)(v), an applicant must demonstrate that refusing to admit him or her to the United States would result in extreme hardship to a citizen or LPR spouse or parent. The term *extreme hardship* is not defined in the INA. In the *Expansion of the Provisional Waiver Program* memorandum, the DHS Secretary directs USCIS to clarify the factors it considers in making a determination about extreme hardship and "to consider criteria by which a presumption of extreme hardship may be determined to exist."

Discussion

This set of executive actions offers different types of immigration relief to different subgroups of the unauthorized population. The beneficiary groups reflect the general priority the U.S. immigration system gives to preserving the unity of the immediate families of U.S. citizens and LPRs. None of the executive actions directly grant beneficiaries a lawful immigration status – only congressional action can confer immigration status.

The expansion of the provisional unlawful presence waiver program to specified relatives of U.S. citizens and LPRs—spouses and minor children of LPRs and adult children of U.S. citizens and LPRs—with approved immigrant visa petitions could help facilitate these individuals' acquisition of LPR status. Beneficiaries of approved immigrant petitions who are unable to adjust status in the United States would still need to return to their home countries in order to pursue LPR status. Before leaving the United States to apply for a visa abroad, however, an eligible individual could apply for and receive a provisional unlawful presence waiver. During the overseas visa process, if a consular officer determines that the individual is subject to a 3- or 10-year bar on admission—and that no other grounds of inadmissibility apply—the individual could use the waiver to obtain a visa and gain admission to the United States as an LPR.

The executive action on advance parole also addresses the 3- and 10-year bars, but in a different way. It effectively would make the 3- and 10-year bars inapplicable in cases in which an individual leaves the United States after being granted advance parole and then seeks to return.

The expansion of the military parole-in-place program would enable eligible spouses, children, and parents of U.S. citizens and LPRs who seek to enlist in the U.S. Armed Forces to be granted parole. Although parole is not considered an immigration status, an individual with parole can adjust to LPR status in the United States provided that he or she meets the applicable requirements (see "Provisional Unlawful Presence Waivers").

The expansion of eligibility for DACA and the establishment of a new deferred action process for the unauthorized parents of U.S. citizens and LPRs who meet specified requirements could enable individuals in the newly covered groups to remain in the United States and, if granted employment authorization, to work legally. During the period of deferred action, these individuals would have protection from removal. They would be in a period of stay authorized by DHS and would be considered to be lawfully present for admissibility purposes. As such, during the period of deferred action, they would not accrue unlawful presence for admissibility purposes (which is relevant for application of the 3- and 10-year bars). Individuals granted deferred action would not be provided with a pathway to a lawful immigration status, however, and DHS has the discretion to terminate the grant of deferred action at any time.

HIGH-SKILLED WORKERS

A key principle underlying U.S. immigration policy is facilitating the permanent and temporary entry of foreign nationals with needed skills.

Admitting professional, managerial, and skilled foreign workers raises a series of policy tensions as the United States attempts to compete internationally for the most talented workers without negatively impacting wages and working conditions of native workers and students entering the U.S. labor market.[76]

Permanent Employment-Based Immigration[77]

Immigrant admissions and adjustments for LPR status are subject to a complex set of numerical limits and preference categories that give priority for admission on the basis of family relationships, needed skills, and geographic diversity. The current employment-based LPR visa system consists of five numerically limited preference categories:

- *first preference*: priority workers who are persons of extraordinary ability in the arts, the sciences, education, business, or athletics; outstanding professors and researchers; and certain multinational executives and managers;
- *second preference*: members of the professions holding advanced degrees or persons of exceptional ability;
- *third preference*: skilled workers with at least two years training, professionals with baccalaureate degrees, and unskilled workers in occupations in which U.S. workers are in short supply;
- *fourth preference*: special immigrants who largely consist of religious workers, certain former employees of the U.S. government, and undocumented juveniles who become wards of the court; and
- *fifth preference*: investors who invest at least $1 million (or less money in rural areas or areas of high unemployment) to create at least 10 new jobs.

Employers who seek to hire prospective immigrant workers petition USCIS. Employers who seek to hire prospective employment-based immigrants through the second and third preference categories also must petition the U.S. Department of Labor (DOL) on behalf of the alien (see "Labor Certification" below).[78]

High-Skilled Temporary Worker Visas[79]

Temporary visas for professional, managerial, and skilled foreign workers have become an important gateway for high-skilled permanent immigration to the United States.[80] The Administration contends that employers use temporary worker visas to retain workers as they wait for LPR visa numbers to become available. If workers' nonimmigrant visas expire before their permanent visas become available, such workers must leave the country.[81]

Over the past two decades, the number of visas issued for temporary employment-based workers has more than doubled, from just over 400,000 in FY1994 to over 1 million in FY2013.[82] Notably, policy makers and advocates have focused on two visa categories in particular: H-1B visas for professional specialty workers and L visas for intracompany transferees. These two nonimmigrant visas epitomize the tensions between the global competition for talent and possible adverse effects on U.S. workers.

Changes to Current Policy

On November 20, 2014, the DHS Secretary released a policy memorandum stating that USCIS will be producing new regulations and policies designed to "grow our economy and create jobs" by attracting and retaining highly skilled immigrants.[83] The policy changes will affect employment-based LPR visas; optional practical training (OPT) for foreign students; the L visa category for intracompany transfers; and select foreign nationals who are inventors, researchers, and founders of start-up enterprises.[84] In addition, the Secretary announced that he will be publishing a final rule to incentivize employers of current temporary workers to sponsor them for LPR status. Concurrently, DOL announced a review of the policies and regulations related to labor certification.[85]

Preventing Visa Retrogression[86]

As discussed above, a complex set of numerical limits and preference categories dictate how many and which persons may become LPRs in a given year. DOS is responsible for allocating the visas based on family- and employment-based preference categories and uniform per-country limits. DOS must calculate when a visa number is available for a specific foreign national with an approved immigrant petition, allowing that foreign national to adjust to LPR status if they are in the United States or receive their LPR visa if they are outside the country. Several years ago, "accounting problems" between USCIS's processing of LPR adjustments of status in the United States and Consular Affairs' processing of LPR visas abroad became apparent.[87] This difference unexpectedly lengthened the wait for a visa for some foreign nationals with approved LPR applications (i.e., visa retrogression).[88]

In the High-Skilled Memorandum, the Secretary states that USCIS should continue to work with DOS to make sure that all immigrant visas are allocated when there is demand for such visas, and improve the system for determining when visas become available. DOS reportedly has agreed to modify the visa bulletin to clarify when a person's visa number will become available.

Labor Certification

The INA bars the admission of prospective immigrants who seek to enter the United States to perform skilled or unskilled labor, unless the Secretary of Labor certifies to the Secretaries of State and Homeland Security that such foreign workers will not displace or adversely affect the working conditions of U.S. workers.[89] All labor certification applications (LCAs) for aliens seeking LPR status are processed through DOL's Program Electronic Review Management (PERM) labor certification system.[90] In FY2014, employers reportedly submitted over 70,000 PERM applications requesting foreign workers, and the majority of the job openings were for professional occupations in Information Technology and Science. [91] Under the President's executive action, DOL will review the PERM program and relevant regulations, with the goal of making the program more responsive to changes in the national work force.[92]

Changing Jobs

Currently, employees with pending employment-based LPR visa applications may change jobs without jeopardizing their application only if the new job or position is in a "same or similar" occupational classification. Reportedly, workers often will not accept promotions or change employers due to fear of invalidating their applications.[93] Under the High-Skilled Memorandum, USCIS was directed to consider amending regulations to ensure that long-standing visa petitions are not invalidated in cases where the employee seeks to change jobs or employers. Specifically, the DHS Secretary directed USCIS to issue a policy memorandum that provides guidance on the definition of "same or similar" occupational classification.

National Interest Waiver

Generally, foreign nationals attempting to immigrate under the second and third employment- based preference categories must be sponsored by an employer, who must certify that the foreign national is not displacing U.S. workers. Under the INA, certain foreign nationals with advanced degrees or exceptional ability may apply for LPR status without an employer sponsor if it is in the national interest.[94] This is known as the "national interest waiver."[95] According to the Administration, the waiver is underutilized and limited guidance exists on its use. In the High Skilled Memorandum, the DHS Secretary directs USCIS to issue guidance or regulations clarifying the circumstances under which the national interest waiver can be used.

Start up Visas

Some have criticized the fifth-preference employment-based (EB-5) visa category for not allowing its applicants, who generate business ideas and obtain investor backing to launch them, to petition for LPR status.[96] In the 113th Congress, House-passed H.R. 2131 and Senate-passed S.744 would have, under certain circumstances, allowed foreign nationals who received investment money from qualified investors to apply for LPR status.

The DHS Secretary, through the High-Skilled Memorandum, directs USCIS to create a program using the "significant public benefit" parole authority[97] to allow certain high-skilled foreign nationals to enter or remain in the United States. The program would grant parole on a case-by- case basis to investors, researchers, and founders of start-up enterprises who may not qualify for the public interest waiver or EB-5 status, but who have secured "substantial" financing from U.S. investors or who "otherwise hold the promise of innovation and job creation through the development of new technologies or the pursuit of 'cutting edge' research."

According to the memorandum, the grant of parole would temporarily allow these foreign nationals to pursue research, new ideas, and businesses in the United States rather than abroad, and give them time to secure temporary or permanent immigration statuses. Regulations to implement this program must include income and resource requirements. In addition, those who receive parole under this program will, reportedly, be ineligible for federal public benefits[98] and premium tax credits under the Affordable Care Act.[99]

Optional Practical Training (OPT)

During or after completing their undergraduate or graduate studies, foreign students on F-1 visas are permitted to participate in employment known as Optional Practical Training (OPT).[100] OPT is temporary employment that is directly related to an F-1 student's major area of study.

Generally, an F-1 foreign student may work up to 12 months in OPT status. In 2008, DHS expanded the OPT work period to 29 months for F-1 students in STEM fields.[101]

The High-Skilled Memorandum directs USCIS and ICE to develop regulations to expand the number of degree programs eligible for OPT, and to extend the time period and use of OPT for STEM students and graduates. The new policy will also require the OPT program to have stronger ties to degree-granting institutions to ensure that a student's OPT furthers his or her course of study in the United States. In addition, the new policy is to be consistent with U.S. worker protections.

L Visas[102]

Current law permits intracompany transferees to enter the United States on a nonimmigrant L visa that is designed for executives, managers, or employees with specialized knowledge of a firm's products. The L visa permits multinational firms to transfer top-level personnel to their locations in the United States for up to seven years.[103] The INA does not require firms wishing to bring L intracompany transfers into the United States to demonstrate that U.S. workers will not be adversely affected in order to obtain L visas.

The L visa category is considered essential to retaining and expanding international businesses in the United States. Some, however, have raised concerns that intracompany transferees on the L visa may displace U.S. workers who had been employed in those positions for these firms in the United States. Others contend that the L visa has become a substitute for the H-1B visa, noting that L visa employees are often comparable in skills and occupations to H-1B workers yet lack the latter's labor market protections. These concerns have often been raised with certain outsourcing and information technology firms that employ L visa workers as subcontractors within the United States. A related concern is that the unchecked use of L visas will foster the transfer of STEM and other high-skilled professional jobs overseas.[104] After investigating the L visa, the DHS Inspector General offered this assessment: "That so many foreign workers seem to qualify as possessing specialized knowledge appears to have led to the displacement of American workers, and to what is sometimes called the 'body shop' problem."[105]

In the High-Skilled Memorandum, the DHS Secretary directs USCIS to issue a policy clarifying the meaning of "specialized knowledge" for L visa qualification. Reportedly, the goal of the new policy guidance is to yield more consistent adjudication outcomes.[106]

Discussion

The Administration did not provide details about the proposed policy changes related to high- skilled workers, but rather directed agencies to develop policies and regulations in these areas. Until such details are clarified, the potential impact of the changes remains unclear.

INTEGRATION AND NATURALIZATION

Immigrant Integration

Immigrant integration refers to the process by which immigrants become socially, economically, culturally, and politically integrated into American society.[107] The United States admits for permanent residence, and processes for citizenship, the largest proportion and absolute number of foreign nationals of any other major immigrant-receiving nation. As the foreign-born population in the United States increases—41.3 million persons or 13.1% of the total U.S. population in 2013—federally funded immigrant integration programs take on greater prominence.

Unlike other major immigrant-receiving nations, the United States has no national policy or dedicated executive branch office focused on coordinating immigrant integration efforts across federal agencies.[108] Federal immigrant integration programs take direct and indirect forms. Direct forms include the Department of Education's English Language Acquisition Grants and Migrant Education Programs, and the DHS Office of Citizenship's Immigrant Integration and Citizenship Program. Indirect forms are more numerous and often provide assistance to mostly low-income individuals.[109] States and localities also contend with immigrant integration, particularly in new immigrant destination states. Increasing numbers of states and localities grapple with issues of communication and English language learning as well as law enforcement, education, workforce development, adult literacy, and health access, among others.

Immigration advocates contend that the size and growth of the foreign-born population and the need for greater efficiency and integration among federal and state agencies warrants an executive branch office for immigrant integration.[110] A number of task forces have been convened to address this issue.[111] Immigration advocates contend, however, that such proposals must go farther by establishing a federal office to coordinate and facilitate immigrant integration nationally in a more comprehensive manner.[112] The Senate's comprehensive immigration reform bill, S. 744, included such broader provisions.[113]

The President's executive action establishes an interagency "White House Task Force on New Americans" with two primary objectives: (1) identify, promote, and expand immigrant integration best practices within states and localities; and (2) help determine steps that federal agencies can take to improve their own immigrant integration efforts.[114] Other functions outlined within the action include: providing technical assistance and training; collecting and disseminating related data and information; soliciting recommendations from nonprofit organizations, government officials and other stakeholders; and monitoring equitable access to integration programs. The task force is expected to provide the President with recommendations to further the civic, economic, and linguistic integration of new Americans within four months and an implementation status report within a year.

Encouraging Naturalization

Naturalization, the process that grants U.S. citizenship to LPRs, is often viewed as a milestone for immigrants and a measure of their socioeconomic integration and assimilation to the United States. Practically, naturalized immigrants gain important benefits, including the right to vote, security from deportation in most cases, access to certain public-sector jobs, and the ability to travel with a U.S. passport.[115] U.S. citizens are also advantaged over LPRs for sponsoring relatives to immigrate to the United States.

Despite the clear benefits of U.S. citizenship status over LPR status, millions of LPRs who are eligible to naturalize do not do so. Part of the reason for this may stem from INA requirements for naturalization that include five years of continuous residence in the United States, possession of "good moral character" and English language competency, and the passing of a U.S. government and history examination as part of a naturalization interview.[116]

Naturalization applicants must also pay a fee, which some observers argue hinders LPRs from acquiring citizenship.[117] USCIS currently charges $680 to process naturalization petitions. The fee amount raises several issues for Congress, including whether it is sufficiently onerous that it discourages naturalization, and whether it accurately reflects USCIS's cost to process naturalization applications. Empirical studies suggest that the volume of naturalization petitions filed may be inversely related to the naturalization fee amount,[118] although other factors also explain application volume increases apart from fee increases.[119] Immigration advocates have proposed providing more payment options for naturalization fees and making information about fee waivers more widely known.[120]

The President's executive action directs USCIS to accept credit cards as a payment option for the naturalization fee, in addition to money orders or checks (which are currently the only payment options).[121] The action also directs USCIS to consider the feasibility of a partial fee waiver to the naturalization fee. While USCIS offers waivers for some of its immigration services fees, waivers for the $680 naturalization fee are currently available only to those whose income is less than or equal to 150% of the federal poverty level. Those with incomes above this level do not qualify for any waiver and must pay the full $680 fee.

Discussion

How the President's creation of the White House Task force on New Americans marks a significant departure from previous federal efforts that explicitly focused on immigrant integration is unclear. Because it originates from an executive action, it lacks funding from Congress. While some advances may result from greater federal coordination, the actual integration of immigrants into American society—economically, politically, socially, and culturally—involves considerable time and effort across many policy areas. Some immigration observers, citing experiences of earlier generations of immigrants, argue that taxpayers should not be funding government initiatives to foster integration. Others view some integration programs, such as English language instruction, as valuable investments that yield positive long-term returns.

Promoting naturalization generally has wide support, and expanding payment options for the naturalization fee may provide greater convenience for potential naturalization petitioners. Empirical evidence also suggests that the propensity to naturalize is price sensitive, suggesting that naturalization fee waiver options may boost naturalization rates among those who otherwise would not apply. Any such waiver options, however, will require USCIS to make up the corresponding shortfall in fee revenue through other means, including, possibly, reducing services, increasing processing times, and increasing other processing fees.

OTHER EXECUTIVE ACTION INITIATIVES

Modernizing the U.S. Immigrant Visa System

Many agree that the U.S. immigration system contains dysfunctions for those who petition for immigration services and benefits: it is complicated to understand, redundant, time-consuming, and costly and burdensome to applicants and businesses. Some argue that the system, which requires technological infrastructure beyond what its fee structure can support,[122] has reached a level that thwarts effective administration.[123]

Bureaucratic and legal complexity can be expected of an administrative, technical, and legal system that handles the range of immigrant circumstances found in the United States, as well as the corresponding range of goals and objectives of agencies charged with implementing and enforcing U.S. immigration law. Yet, unlike regularly proposed and attempted overhauls of the similarly complex tax system, no major attempts have been made to overhaul the U.S. immigration system to allow it to work more efficiently and expediently.[124]

USCIS, the DHS agency responsible for processing and adjudicating immigration petitions, has for several years undertaken a "modernization" program intended to convert itself from an entirely paper-based agency to a mostly digital platform. A recent review by DHS's Office of the Inspector General suggested that the program's goals have not yet been met.[125]

On November 21, the White House, as part of the President's executive action, directed the Secretaries of State and Homeland Security in consultation with other federal agencies and stakeholders to recommend ways to (1) improve and streamline the legal immigration system, emphasizing reforms that reduce government costs, improve services for applicants, reduce employer burdens, and reduce waste and fraud; (2) ensure that all the visa numbers are used; and (3) modernize the visa processing technology to reduce redundancy, improve applicants' experiences and increase public oversight. The secretaries are also to establish metrics that can quantify improvement in these three areas.[126]

Such reforms, long desired, will become more critical for USCIS as it implements the President's executive action. Soliciting recommendations for improving the functioning of the immigration system may help alleviate some challenges faced by end users. As with other components of the President's initiative, it remains to be seen how much can be accomplished through administrative refinements and the deployment of existing resources without the benefit of additional funding.

More Consistent Enforcement of Federal Labor, Employment, and Immigration Laws

In 2012, an estimated 8.1 million unauthorized aliens, representing just over 5% of the U.S. workforce, were working or looking for work in the United States.[127] Lacking proper work authorization, they are vulnerable to exploitation in a variety of ways and less likely to have sufficient resources to enforce their rights effectively.[128]

Three sources of labor protections exist for foreign workers in the United States: (1) conditions imposed on employers hiring foreign workers through the labor certification-attestation portion of the petition to admit foreign workers; (2) federal labor laws regarding employer adherence to requirements for wages and working conditions; and (3) private causes of action that foreign workers may have under state and local laws.[129] DOL, which is responsible for enforcing minimum wage, overtime pay, and related requirements, focuses a significant percentage of its enforcement resources on low-wage industries that employ large numbers of immigrant—and presumably large numbers of unauthorized—workers.[130] Among other tasks, ICE is responsible for investigating immigration law violations related to knowingly hiring unauthorized aliens.[131]

In April 2009, DHS issued new guidance on immigration-related worksite enforcement that "reflects a renewed Department-wide focus targeting criminal aliens and employers who cultivate illegal workplaces by breaking the country's laws and knowingly hiring illegal workers."[132] In December 2011, DHS and DOL signed a revised memorandum of understanding to coordinate worksite enforcement actions and make them consistent with each agency's mission.[133] Questions have arisen as to how rigorous and effective DHS's worksite enforcement efforts are and have been in past years.[134]

On November 21, 2014, as part of the President's executive action, DOL announced the creation of an inter-agency working group to "promote effective and consistent enforcement of federal labor, employment, and immigration laws, with the goal of protecting all workers regardless of legal status."[135] The working group will include representatives from federal agencies responsible for immigration enforcement and worker protections, including the Departments of Labor, Homeland Security, and Justice, and the

Equal Employment Opportunity Commission and National Labor Relations Board.

The working group is broadly tasked with ensuring that (1) current immigration and employment policies do not dissuade workers from cooperating with law enforcement authorities in cases of employment violations; (2) federal enforcement authorities are not used by those who wish to undermine worker protections by enmeshing immigration authorities in labor disputes; and (3) federal labor, employment, and immigration laws are consistently applied.

As with most of the other elements of the President's executive action, this initiative is being implemented without a congressional appropriation or stated source of funding. Hence, it remains to be seen the extent to which the creation of an inter-agency task force and greater coordination and planning among and within agencies can improve wages and worksite conditions for workers vulnerable to exploitation because of their immigration status (or lack thereof).

Expanding Support for Crime Victims

U nonimmigrant status is reserved for victims of certain statutorily specified crimes that occurred within the United States.[136] To qualify for U status, a foreign national must receive certification from a law enforcement agency that he or she is being or is likely to be helpful in the investigation and prosecution of the criminal activity.

T nonimmigrant status is reserved for foreign nationals in the United States who are victims of severe forms of trafficking. To receive it, foreign nationals, with some exceptions, must comply with reasonable requests for assistance from law enforcement. Law enforcement certification is optional for T status, unlike for U status, but it serves as important evidence for applicants.[137]

As part of the President's executive actions, the Department of Labor (DOL) has announced that in early 2015 it will begin exercising its authority to provide law enforcement certification to trafficking victims applying for T status.[138] In addition, DOL will simultaneously expand the types of crimes for which it certifies to include victims of extortion, forced labor, and foreign labor contracting fraud.[139]

The DOL Wage and Hour Division enforces federal labor laws, including the Fair Labor Standards Act and the Migrant and Seasonal Agricultural

Workers Protection Act, and assists with human trafficking investigations involving violations of these laws. As a result, DOL may encounter trafficking victims. Some advocates note that DOL's enforcement of wage and hour laws could help reveal trafficking and crime victims, as those who engage in labor trafficking or other criminal activity in the workplace are also likely to violate wage and hour laws.[140]

CONCLUSION

The President's Immigration Accountability Executive Action announced on November 20, 2014, includes provisions meant to alleviate uncertainty for potentially millions of unauthorized aliens through deferred action and the use of provisional waivers and parole. It is also intended to revise enforcement priorities and improve and coordinate strategic initiatives across a range of immigration policy areas, including border security, high skilled immigration, and naturalization. Whether this executive action can accomplish these objectives and prompt Congress to pass more permanent legislative solutions is unclear.

Accomplishing such goals in the face of a potentially resistant Congress may prove challenging. USCIS, the agency tasked with carrying out sizable portions of the executive action, will be relying upon an indeterminate amount of additional fee revenue from deferred action petitions to implement some of these objectives, while other agencies, lacking congressional appropriations, will be attempting to implement changes to current policies and procedures mostly through increased coordination and more innovative marshaling of existing resources.

End Notes

1 Migration Policy Institute, *MPI: As Many as 3.7 Million Unauthorized Immigrants Could Get Relief from Deportation under Anticipated New Deferred Action Program - With Existing DACA Program Included, Anticipated Actions Could Benefit More than 5.2 Million in Total — Nearly Half of U.S. Unauthorized Population*, Press Release, November 30, 2014. The press release is based upon analytic work presented in Randy Capps, Marc R. Rosenblum, and James D. Bachmeier, *Executive Action for Unauthorized Immigrants: Estimates of the Populations that Could Receive Relief*, Migration Policy Institute, Issue Brief No. 10, Washington, DC, September 2014.

2 For more information on this debate, see CRS Report R43782, *Executive Discretion as to Immigration: Legal Overview*, by Kate M. Manuel and Michael John Garcia.

[3] For example, see a discussion of broad immigration debates surrounding family-based immigration in CRS Report R43145, *U.S. Family-Based Immigration Policy*, by William A. Kandel.

[4] CRS Report R41207, *Unauthorized Aliens in the United States: Policy Discussion*, by Andorra Bruno.

[5] See archived CRS Report R42530, *Immigration of Foreign Nationals with Science, Technology, Engineering, and Mathematics (STEM) Degrees* , by Ruth Ellen Wasem.

[6] CRS Report R42866, *Permanent Legal Immigration to the United States: Policy Overview*, by William A. Kandel.

[7] CRS Report R42969, *Border Security: Understanding Threats at U.S. Borders*, by Jerome P. Bjelopera and Kristin Finklea; CRS Report R43356, *Border Security: Immigration Inspections at Ports of Entry*, by Lisa Seghetti; CRS Report R42138, *Border Security: Immigration Enforcement Between Ports of Entry*, by Lisa Seghetti; CRS Report R42057, *Interior Immigration Enforcement: Programs Targeting Criminal Aliens*, by Marc R. Rosenblum and William A. Kandel.

[8] In the 113th Congress, House committees reported or ordered to be reported the following immigration bills: Border Security Results Act of 2013 (H.R. 1417); Strengthen and Fortify Enforcement (SAFE) Act (H.R. 2278); Legal Workforce Act (H.R. 1772); Agricultural Guestworker (AG) Act (H.R. 1773); and Supplying Knowledge-based Immigrants and Lifting Levels of STEM Visas (SKILLS Visa) Act (H.R. 2131).

[9] For more information, see CRS Report R42138, *Border Security: Immigration Enforcement Between Ports of Entry*, by Lisa Seghetti.

[10] These include a network of ground sensors, agent-centric mobile surveillance equipment, integrated fixed towers, agent-portable tripod-mounted surveillance systems, vehicle-mounted mobile surveillance systems, truck-mounted mobile vehicle surveillance systems, tower-mounted remote video surveillance systems, and air-based surveillance systems, all of which are linked, to varying degrees, to centralized control rooms where personnel monitor the border, alert field agents to potential incursions, and coordinate the response. In recent years, the Border Patrol's focus with respect to surveillance technology has shifted from fixed towers and other static resources to more mobile and dynamic systems. From CRS discussions with U.S. Border Patrol, December 17, 2012 and August 26, 2014; also see U.S. Border Patrol, *2012-2016 Border Patrol Strategic Plan*, Washington, DC: 2012.

[11] CBP houses much of this capacity in its "Office of Air and Marine. . .[which] is the world's largest aviation and maritime law enforcement organization, a critical component of CBP's layered enforcement strategy for border security. [The Office of Air and Marine has] 1,200 federal agents, more than 250 aircraft and over 280 marine vessels operating from 83 locations in the United States and Puerto Rico. See http://www.cbp.gov/border-security/air-sea.

[12] This includes items such as fencing and lighting along the border. In addition to fencing and other infrastructure in the immediate border region, DHS deploys a variety of checkpoints and forward operating bases to enhance border security. Checkpoints, including permanent and "tactical" (or roving) checkpoints, are located at some distance from the linear border, usually within 100 miles of the border.

[13] See for example, Jeh Charles Johnson, Secretary, Department of Homeland Security, "Border Security in the 21st Century," public remarks delivered at the Center for Strategic and International Studies, Washington, D.C., October 9, 2014. Hereafter Johnson, "Border Security in the 21st Century." White House, "Fixing the Immigration System for America's 21st Century Economy."

[14] See, for example, Tom Howell, Jr, "Senate Republicans: Immigration Reform Must Deal First with Border Security," *Washington Times,* November 19, 2014; Alan Gomez, "Border Security Quandary Could Kill Immigration Bill," *USA Today*, April 2, 2013.

[15] Johnson, "Border Security in the 21st Century."

[16] CBP, *2012-2016 Border Patrol Strategic Plan*, Washington, DC: 2012, p. 7.

[17] Ibid.

[18] Office of Air and Marine and the Office of Field Operations (CBP officers at POEs).

[19] Joint written testimony of Custom and Border Protection's U.S. Border Patrol Chief Michael Fisher, (then) Office of Air and Marine Assistant Commissioner Michael Kostelnik, Office of Technology Innovation & Acquisition Assistant Commissioner Mark Borkowski, and (then) Office of Field Operations Acting Assistant Commissioner Kevin McAleenan for a House Committee on Appropriations, Subcommittee on Homeland Security hearing on The President's Fiscal Year 2013 budget request for CBP, February 29, 2012.

[20] U.S. Department of Homeland Security, Memorandum to R. Gil Kerlikowske, Commissioner, U.S. Customs and Border Protection, Admiral Paul F. Zukunft, Commandant, U.S. Coast Guard, Thomas S. Winkowski, Acting Director, U.S. Immigration and Customs Enforcement, Leon Rodriquez, Director, U.S. Citizenship and Immigration Services, W. Craig Fugate, Administrator, Federal Emergency Management Agency, and Alan D. Bersin, Acting Assistant Secretary for Policy, from Jeh Charles Johnson, Secretary of Homeland Security, *Southern Border and Approaches Campaign*, November 20, 2014.

[21] Ibid.

[22] According to the November 20, 2014 memo, the Task Forces "should adopt a supported-supporting component model. Among the Components of this Department [DHS], CBP will be the supported component in Joint Task Force West, the USCG will be the supported component in Joint Task Force East, and ICE will be the supported component in Joint Task Force Investigations."

[23] In the civil immigration enforcement context, the term "prosecutorial discretion" applies to a broad range of discretionary enforcement decisions including issuing or canceling notices to appear (NTAs) which start the removal process, allowing other forms of removal (e.g., voluntary departure), rather than instituting a standard removal proceeding in immigration court, granting deferred action and deciding whom to arrest for a violation of civil immigration law. Prosecutorial discretion may be exercised at any stage of an enforcement proceeding, but policy states that it should generally be exercised as early in the case as possible to preserve government resources.

[24] DHS personnel who are authorized to initiate removal procedures include U.S. Customs and Border Protection (CBP) officers and U.S. Border Patrol agents (within CBP), asylum and examination officers in U.S. Citizenship and Immigration Services (USCIS), and detention officers and other agents in U.S. Immigration and Customs Enforcement (ICE); see 8 C.F.R. §239.1(a).

[25] U.S. Department of Homeland Security, Memorandum to Thomas S. Winkowski, Acting Director, U.S. Immigration and Customs Enforcement, R. Gil Kerlikowske, Commissioner, U.S. Customs and Border Protection, Leon Rodriquez, Director, U.S. Citizenship and Immigration Services, and Alan D. Bersin, Acting Assistant Secretary for Policy, from Jeh Charles Johnson, Secretary of Homeland Security, *Policies for the Apprehension, Detention, and Removal of Undocumented Immigrants*, November 20, 2014; and U.S. Department of Homeland Security, Memorandum to Thomas S. Winkowski, Acting Director, U.S. Immigration and Customs Enforcement, Megan Mack, Officer, Officer of Civil Rights and Civil Liberties, and Philip A. McNamara, Assistant Secretary, Intergovernmental Affairs, from Jeh Charles Johnson, Secretary of Homeland Security, *Secure Communities*, November 20, 2014.

[26] U.S. Department of Homeland Security, Memorandum to Thomas S. Winkowski, Acting Director, U.S. Immigration and Customs Enforcement, and Catherine Emerson, Chief Human Capital Officer, Department of Homeland Security, from Jeh Charles Johnson, Secretary of Homeland Security, *Personnel Reform for Immigration and Customs Enforcement Officers*, November 20, 2014.

[27] U.S. Department of Homeland Security, Memorandum to Thomas S. Winkowski, Acting Director, U.S. Immigration and Customs Enforcement, R. Gil Kerlikowske, Commissioner, U.S. Customs and Border Protection, Leon Rodriquez, Director, U.S. Citizenship and

Immigration Services, and Alan D. Bersin, Acting Assistant Secretary for Policy, from Jeh Charles Johnson, Secretary of Homeland Security, *Policies for the Apprehension, Detention, and Removal of Undocumented Immigrants*, November 20, 2014, p. 2.

[28] Criminal street gang is defined in 18 U.S.C. §521(a).

[29] Felonies include any offense classified as a felony in the convicting jurisdiction, and any aggravated felony as defined in INA §101(a)(43).

[30] This excludes traffic offenses.

[31] Significant misdemeanor is defined as an offense of domestic violence, sexual abuse or exploitation; burglary; unlawful possession or use of a firearm; drug distribution or trafficking; or driving under the influence; or one for which the individual was sentenced to time in custody for 90 days or more.

[32] The policy leaves room for discretion among DHS personnel, even with *Priority 1* aliens. The policy states that an alien should be prioritized for removal unless he or she may be eligible for relief from removal or factors exist that, in the judgment of DHS personnel, indicate the person should not be an enforcement priority. Notably, *Priority 1* requires "compelling and exceptional factors that clearly indicate the alien is not a threat to national security, border security, or public safety and should not therefore be an enforcement priority," while *Priority 3* requires "the alien is not a threat to the integrity of the immigration system or there are factors suggesting the alien should not be an enforcement priority."

[33] John Morton, *Memorandum on Civil Immigration Enforcement: Priorities for the Apprehension, Detention, and Removal of Aliens*, U.S. Immigration and Customs Enforcement, Washington, DC, March 2, 2011; John Morton, *Exercising Prosecutorial Discretion Consistent with the Civil Immigration Enforcement Priorities of the Agency for the Apprehension, Detention, and Removal of Aliens*, U.S. Department of Homeland Security Immigration and Customs Enforcement, Washington, DC, June 17, 2011; and John Morton, *Prosecutorial Discretion: Certain Victims, Witnesses, and Plaintiffs*, U.S. Department of Homeland Security Immigration and Customs Enforcement, Washington, DC, June 17, 2011.

[34] Although the immigration agencies have issued guidance regarding enforcement priorities since at least 1975, analysis of the evolution of enforcement priorities is beyond the scope of this report.

[35] Aliens who have been issued final orders of removal but who have not departed from the United States are known as absconders or fugitive aliens. Since FY2002, there has been a concerted effort to remove absconders. In 2003, Congress mandated that the names of absconders be added to DOJ's National Crime Information System. See archived CRS Report RL33351, *Immigration Enforcement Within the United States*, coordinated by Alison Siskin, and CRS Report R42057, *Interior Immigration Enforcement: Programs Targeting Criminal Aliens*, by Marc R. Rosenblum and William A. Kandel.

[36] John Morton, *Memorandum on Civil Immigration Enforcement: Priorities for the Apprehension, Detention, and Removal of Aliens*, U.S. Immigration and Customs Enforcement, Washington, DC, March 2, 2011.

[37] Under statute, those subject to mandatory detention include criminal aliens, national security risks, certain arriving aliens, and select persons with final orders of removal. For more on mandatory detention, see CRS Report RL32369, *Immigration-Related Detention*, by Alison Siskin, and CRS Report WSLG524, *How "Mandatory" Is the Mandatory Detention of Certain Aliens in Removal Proceedings,* by Michael John Garcia.

[38] For example, see Mark Hugo Lopez, Ana Gonzalez-Barrera, and Seth Motel, *As Deportations Rise to Record Levels, Most Latinos Oppose Obama's Policy*, Pew Research Hispanic Trends Project, Washington, DC, December 28, 2011, Appendix A.

[39] For example, see Jessica Vaughan, *Deportation Numbers Unwrapped: Raw Statistics Reveal the Real Story of ICE Enforcement in Decline*, Center for Immigration Studies, Washington, DC, October 2013; and Brian Bennett, "High Deportation Figures are Misleading," *LA Times*, April 1, 2014, p. 1.

[40] Chuck Wexler et al., *Taskforce on Secure Communities Findings and Recommendations*, Homeland Security Advisory Council, Washington, DC, September 2011, p. 11; and ICE, *Congressional Budget Justification FY2014*, p. 57.

[41] DOJ's Integrated Automated Fingerprint Identification System (IAFIS) conducts criminal and terrorist background checks in response to requests from federal, state, and local law enforcement agencies by checking fingerprints against the IAFIS database of fingerprints, criminal histories, photographs, and biographic information. See Federal Bureau of Investigation, "Integrated Automated Fingerprint Identification System," http://www.fbi.gov/about-us/cjis/ fingerprints_biometrics/iafis/iafis.

[42] The IDENT database is DHS's primary department-wide biometric database, and includes photographs, fingerprints, biographic name, personal identifier data, citizenship and nationality, and derogatory information, if applicable. See DHS, *Privacy Impact Assessment for the Automated Biometric Identification System (IDENT),* Dec. 7, 2012.

[43] Chuck Wexler et al., *Taskforce on Secure Communities Findings and Recommendations*, Homeland Security Advisory Council, Washington, DC, September 2011, p. 10.

[44] The Criminal Alien Program (CAP) is an umbrella program that includes several different systems for identifying, detaining, and initiating removal proceedings against criminal aliens incarcerated within federal, state, and local prisons and jails, as well as at-large criminal aliens that have been released into communities after serving their sentences. Immigration and Customs Enforcement, Enforcement and Removal Operations, *Crimnal Alien Program*, Fact Sheet, Washington, DC, http://www.ice.gov/ criminal-alien-program. See also CRS Report R42057, *Interior Immigration Enforcement: Programs Targeting Criminal Aliens*, by Marc R. Rosenblum and William A. Kandel.

[45] U.S. Department of Homeland Security, Memorandum to Thomas S. Winkowski, Acting Director, U.S. Immigration and Customs Enforcement, Megan Mack, Officer, Office of Civil Rights and Civil Liberties, and Philip A. McNamara, Assistant Secretary for Intergovernmental Affairs, from Jeh Charles Johnson, Secretary of Homeland Security, *Secure Communities*, November 20, 2014.

[46] ICE and its predecessor, the Immigration and Naturalization Service (INS), have used detainers as one means of obtaining custody of aliens for removal proceedings since at least 1950. CRS Report R42690, *Immigration Detainers: Legal Issues*, by Kate M. Manuel.

[47] See CRS Report R42690, *Immigration Detainers: Legal Issues*, by Kate M. Manuel.

[48] Chuck Wexler et al., *Taskforce on Secure Communities Findings and Recommendations*, Homeland Security Advisory Council, Washington, DC, September 2011, p. 26.

[49] U.S. Department of Homeland Security, Memorandum to Thomas S. Winkowski, Acting Director, U.S. Immigration and Customs Enforcement, and Catherine Emerson, Chief Human Capital Officer, Department of Homeland Security, from Jeh Charles Johnson, Secretary of Homeland Security, *Personnel Reform for Immigration and Customs Enforcement Officers*, November 20, 2014, p. 2.

[50] Ibid, p. 1.

[51] Dan Cadman, *Analysis of Obama's Executive Amnesty Scheme: ICE Personnel Reform*, Center for Immigration Studies, Washington, DC, December 2, 2014.

[52] Aliens who have been issued final orders of removal but who have not departed from the United States are known as absconders or fugitive aliens. In 2003, Congress mandated that the names of absconders be added to DOJ's National Crime Information System. See archived CRS Report RL33351, *Immigration Enforcement Within the United States*, coordinated by Alison Siskin, and CRS Report R42057, *Interior Immigration Enforcement: Programs Targeting Criminal Aliens*, by Marc R. Rosenblum and William A. Kandel.

[53] ICE, *Congressional Budget Justification FY2015*, pp. 52-53.

[54] *Alien* is a term in U.S. immigration law that is synonymous with *foreign national* and *noncitizen*.

[55] See CRS Report RL33863, *Unauthorized Alien Students: Issues and "DREAM Act" Legislation*, by Andorra Bruno.

[56] Border Security, Economic Opportunity, and Immigration Modernization Act (S. 744). See CRS Report R43097, *Comprehensive Immigration Reform in the 113th Congress: Major Provisions in Senate-Passed S. 744*, by Ruth Ellen Wasem. CRS Report R43782, *Executive Discretion as to Immigration: Legal Overview*, by Kate M. Manuel and Michael John Garcia.

[57] For a discussion of related legal issues, see CRS Report R43798, *The Obama Administration's November 2014 Immigration Initiatives: Questions and Answers*, by Kate M. Manuel; and CRS Report R43782, *Executive Discretion as to Immigration: Legal Overview*, by Kate M. Manuel and Michael John Garcia.

[58] U.S. Department of Homeland Security, U.S. Citizenship and Immigration Services, Consideration of Deferred Action for Childhood Arrivals Process, Frequently Asked Questions, http://www.uscis.gov/humanitarian/consideration-deferred-action-childhood-arrivals- process/frequently-asked-questions. For additional information on prosecutorial discretion and deferred action, see CRS Report R43782, *Executive Discretion as to Immigration: Legal Overview*, by Kate M. Manuel and Michael John Garcia, and CRS Report R42924, *Prosecutorial Discretion in Immigration Enforcement: Legal Issues*, by Kate M. Manuel and Todd Garvey.

[59] U.S. Department of Homeland Security, Memorandum to David V. Aguilar, Acting Commissioner, U.S. Customs and Border Protection, Alejandro Mayorkas, Director, U.S. Citizenship and Immigration Services, John Morton, Director, U.S. Immigration and Customs Enforcement, from Janet Napolitano, Secretary of Homeland Security, Exercising Prosecutorial Discretion with Respect to Individuals Who Came to the United States as Children, June 15, 2012.

[60] See CRS Report R43747, *Deferred Action for Childhood Arrivals (DACA): Frequently Asked Questions*, by Andorra Bruno.

[61] U.S. Department of Homeland Security, Memorandum to Leon Rodriguez, Director, U.S. Citizenship and Immigration Services, Thomas S. Winkowski, Acting Director, U.S. Immigration and Customs Enforcement, R. Gil Kerlikowske, Commissioner, U.S. Customs and Border Protection, from Jeh Charles Johnson, Secretary of Homeland Security, *Exercising Prosecutorial Discretion with Respect to Individuals Who Came to the United States as Children and with Respect to Certain Individuals Whose Parents are U.S. Citizens or Permanent Residents*, November 20, 2014.

[62] U.S. Department of Homeland Security, Memorandum to Leon Rodriguez, Director, U.S. Citizenship and Immigration Services, from Jeh Charles Johnson, Secretary of Homeland Security, *Families of U.S. Armed Forces Members and Enlistees*, November 20, 2014.

[63] INA §212(d)(5)(A).

[64] Individuals previously lawfully admitted to the United States, even if no longer in a lawful immigration status, are not considered eligible for parole. For this reason, as discussed above, the memorandum directs USCIS to consider the availability of deferred action for unauthorized family members of military service members and veterans who were previously lawfully admitted to the United States.

[65] See U.S. Department of Homeland Security, U.S. Citizenship and Immigration Services, *Parole of Spouses, Children and Parents of Active Duty Members of the U.S. Armed Forces, the Selected Reserve of the Ready Reserve, and Former Members of the U.S. Armed Forces or Selected Reserve of the Ready Reserve and the Effect of Parole on Inadmissibility under Immigration and Nationality Act § 2 l 2(a)(6)(A)(i)*, November 15, 2013.

[66] U.S. Department of Homeland Security, Memorandum to Leon Rodriguez, Director, U.S. Citizenship and Immigration Services, from Jeh Charles Johnson, Secretary of Homeland Security, *Families of U.S. Armed Forces Members and Enlistees*, November 20, 2014.

[67] The Board of Immigration Appeals in the Department of Justice is the highest administrative body for interpreting and applying immigration laws. BIA decisions are binding on all DHS officers and immigration judges unless modified or overruled by the Attorney General or a federal court.

[68] The INA enumerates grounds of inadmissibility—grounds upon which aliens are ineligible for visas and admission to the United States. For an overview of the INA grounds of inadmissibility, see CRS Report R43589, *Immigration: Visa Security Policies*, by Ruth Ellen Wasem, p. 5.

[69] U.S. Department of Homeland Security, Memorandum to Stevan E.Bunnell, General Counsel, Office of the General Counsel, Leon Rodriguez, Director, U.S. Citizenship and Immigration Services, Thomas S. Winkowski, Acting Director, U.S. Immigration and Customs Enforcement, R. Gil Kerlikowske, Commissioner, U.S. Customs and Border Protection, from Jeh Charles Johnson, Secretary of Homeland Security, *Directive to Provide Consistency Regarding Advance Parole*, November 20, 2014.

[70] See CRS Report R42866, *Permanent Legal Immigration to the United States: Policy Overview*, by William A. Kandel.

[71] There is no statutory restriction on submitting a visa petition on behalf of an alien who is in the United States without a lawful immigration status.

[72] INA §245(a).

[73] Spouses and minor children of U.S. citizens and parents of adult U.S. citizens, designated as "immediate relatives" under the family-based immigration system, do not have to wait for a visa number to become available. Other family-based immigrants are subject to a complex set of preference categories and numerical limits, and must wait for an immigrant visa number to be immediately available before they can apply for a visa..

[74] For example, there is an exception for the spouses and children of U.S. citizens and the parents of adult U.S. citizens (INA §245(c)). Another provision (INA §245(i)), which was last updated in 2000, enables aliens who entered the United States unlawfully to adjust status provided they meet other requirements. Among the requirements, the alien must be the beneficiary of a petition or application filed by April 30, 2001.

[75] U.S. Department of Homeland Security, Memorandum to Leon Rodriguez, Director, U.S. Citizenship and Immigration Services, from Jeh Charles Johson, Secretary of Homeland Security, *Expansion of the Provisional Waiver Program*, November 20, 2014.

[76] CRS Report R43745, *Temporary Professional, Managerial, and Skilled Foreign Workers: Legislation in the 113th Congress*, by Ruth Ellen Wasem.

[77] This section is adapted from archived CRS Report RL33977, *Immigration of Foreign Workers: Labor Market Tests and Protections*, by Ruth Ellen Wasem.

[78] Certain second preference immigrants whose admittance is deemed to be "in the national interest" are exempt from labor certification.

[79] This section is adapted from CRS Report R43735, *Temporary Professional, Managerial, and Skilled Foreign Workers: Policy and Trends*, by Ruth Ellen Wasem.

[80] Temporary visas are issued for an expressed purpose and a specific period of time. In most cases, the foreign national must demonstrate they have a "home they have no intention of abandoning" in their native country. For more background on temporary visas, see archived CRS Report RL31381, *U.S. Immigration Policy on Temporary Admissions*, by Ruth Ellen Wasem.

[81] U.S. Department of Homeland Security, Memorandum to Leon Rodriquez, Director, U.S. Citizenship and Immigration Services, and Thomas S. Winkowski, Acting Director, U.S. Immigration and Customs Enforcement, from Jeh Charles Johnson, Secretary of Homeland Security, *Policies Supporting U.S. High-Skilled Business and Workers*, November 20, 2014, p. 2.

[82] While the data include some unskilled and low-skilled workers as well as accompanying family members, visas for managerial, skilled, and professional workers dominate the trends. These data understate the trends in professional, managerial, and skilled foreign workers, because the State Department does not issue visas to nonimmigrants that change status within the United States. For example, a foreign national residing in the United States as a student may convert their status to a temporary nonimmigrant worker without going

abroad to obtain a new visa. Bureau of Consular Affairs, *Report of the Visa Office*, U.S. Department of State, Table XVI, multiple years.

[83] U.S. Department of Homeland Security, Memorandum to Leon Rodriquez, Director, U.S. Citizenship and Immigration Services, and Thomas S. Winkowski, Acting Director, U.S. Immigration and Customs Enforcement, from Jeh Charles Johnson, Secretary of Homeland Security, *Policies Supporting U.S. High-Skilled Business and Workers*, November 20, 2014 (hereafter, "the High-Skilled Memorandum").

[84] Previously, the Administration announced other policies with the goal of retaining high-skilled workers. For example, in May 2014, DHS published a proposed rule to grant work authorization to spouses of H-1B visa holders with approved petitions for LPR status. Department of Homeland Security, U.S. Citizenship and Immigration Services, "Employment Authorization for Certain H-4 Dependent Spouses," 79 *Federal Register* 26886-26901, May 12, 2014.

[85] Department of Labor, *Department of Labor to Pursue Modernized Recruitment and Application Requirements for the PERM Program*, Fact Sheet, Washington, DC, November 20, 2014.

[86] This section is adapted from CRS Report R42048, *Numerical Limits on Employment-Based Immigration: Analysis of the Per-Country Ceilings*, by Ruth Ellen Wasem.

[87] Ibid.

[88] Visa retrogression occurs when visa priority dates moved backward in time rather than forward in time. Most recently, in October 2014, a visa retrogression occurred in the second employment-based preference category for India. See Department of State, *Visa Bulletin, Immigrant Numbers for November 2014*, Washington, DC, October 9, 2014.

[89] INA §212(a)(5). *Labor certification* generally refers to the process in which employers must *document* in the application that certain conditions have been met, including that the employer has attempted to recruit of U.S. workers. As part of this process, the employer must also document the wages, working conditions, and benefits to be provided to foreign workers, thereby permitting DOL to certify that those conditions have been met. *Labor attestation* refers to a process in which employers *attest* that such conditions have been met but do not have to submit documentation with the application. Employers instead must retain documentation showing that the necessary conditions have been satisfied. For more information, see CRS Report R43223, *The Framework for Foreign Workers' Labor Protections Under Federal Law*, by Margaret Mikyung Lee and Jon O. Shimabukuro.

[90] The Program Electronic Review Management (PERM) regulations were published on December 27, 2004, after initially being proposed in May 2002. The stated goals of PERM are to streamline the labor certification process and reduce fraudulent filings. *Federal Register*, vol. 69, no. 247, Dec. 27, 2004, p. 77325.

[91] Department of Labor, *Department of Labor to Pursue Modernized Recruitment and Application Requirements for the PERM Program*, Fact Sheet, Washington, DC, November 20, 2014.

[92] Specifically DOL will seek input on: options for identifying labor force shortages and surpluses and methods for aligning domestic worker recruitment requirements with demonstrated shortages and surpluses; methods to modernize the U.S. worker recruitment requirement; processes to clarify employer obligations to insure PERM positions are fully open to U.S. workers; ranges of processing times and possibilities for premium processing; and the application submission and review process. *Ibid.*

[93] The High-Skilled Memorandum, p. 5.

[94] INA §203(b)(2)(B).

[95] Because no statutory or regulatory definition of "national interest" exists, USCIS relies on a 1998 Administrative Appeals Office precedent decision setting forth a three-prong test for evaluating requests for a national interest waiver. See Matter of New York State Department of Transportation, 22 I&N Dec. 215 (Comm'r 1998) ("NYSDOT"). U.S. Citizenship and Immigration Services, *National Interest Waiver*, Washington, DC.

[96] For an example of this argument, see Amar Toor, "Can Obama's immigration reform stop Silicon Valley's brain drain?," *The Verge*, January 30, 2013. Under the EB-5 category, the money invested by the foreign national must be legally owned by the investor. Matter of Ho, 22 I&N Dec. 206 (Assoc. Comm'r 1998).

[97] INA §212(d)(5).

[98] See CRS Report RL33809, *Noncitizen Eligibility for Federal Public Assistance: Policy Overview and Trends*, by Alison Siskin.

[99] See CRS Report R43561, *Treatment of Noncitizens Under the Affordable Care Act*, by Alison Siskin and Erika K. Lunder.

[100] For more on OPT, see archived CRS Report R42530, *Immigration of Foreign Nationals with Science, Technology, Engineering, and Mathematics (STEM) Degrees* , by Ruth Ellen Wasem.

[101] To qualify for the 17-month extension, F-1 students must have received STEM degrees included on the STEM Designated Degree Program List, be employed by employers enrolled in E-Verify, and have received an initial grant of post-completion OPT related to such a degree (i.e., already approved for 12 months in OPT). 8 C.F.R. 214.2(f)(10). E-Verify is an electronic employment eligibility verification program that U.S. employers voluntarily use to confirm the new hires' employment authorization through Social Security Administration and, if necessary, DHS databases. CRS Report R40446, *Electronic Employment Eligibility Verification*, by Andorra Bruno.

[102] This section is adapted from CRS Report R43745, *Temporary Professional, Managerial, and Skilled Foreign Workers: Legislation in the 113th Congress*, by Ruth Ellen Wasem.

[103] See CRS Report RL33977, *Immigration of Foreign Workers: Labor Market Tests and Protections*, by Ruth Ellen Wasem.

[104] For historical background, see archived CRS Report RL32030, *Immigration Policy for Intracompany Transfers (L Visa): Issues and Legislation*, by Ruth Ellen Wasem.

[105] Office of the Inspector General, *Review of Vulnerabilities and Potential Abuses of the L-1 Visa Program*, U.S. Department of Homeland Security, OIG-06-22, January 2006, p. 9.

[106] U.S. Department of Homeland Security, Memorandum to Leon Rodriquez, Director, U.S. Citizenship and Immigration Services, and Thomas S. Winkowski, Acting Director, U.S. Immigration and Customs Enforcement, from Jeh Charles Johnson, Secretary of Homeland Security, *Policies Supporting U.S. High-Skilled Business and Workers*, November 20, 2014, p. 4.

[107] The term immigrant is synonymous with lawful permanent resident (LPR), a person who has been legally admitted to the United States to reside permanently.

[108] Jeb Bush, Thomas F. McLarty III, and Edward Alden, *U.S. Immigration Policy*, Council on Foreign Relations, Independent Task Force Report No. 63, Washington, DC, 2009, p. 80 (hereafter *U.S. Immigration Policy*, 2009.)

[109] Examples include the Department of Education's Upward Bound Program, which facilitates college enrollment though academic preparation for first-generation college students from low-income families, and the Department of Labor Employment and Training Administration's National Farmworker Jobs Program, which helps seasonal farmworkers and their families attain greater economic stability.

[110] Attempts to create an office can be seen in H.R. 1617 introduced during the 112th Congress which sought to both rename USCIS's Office of Citizenship the Office of Citizenship and Immigrant Integration and to expand its mission accordingly.

[111] In 2006, President George W. Bush initiated the Task Force on New Americans as an inter-agency effort to help immigrants "learn English, embrace the common core of American civic culture, and fully become American." The Task Force worked to develop more cooperative federal approach to assimilation and included representatives from 20 federal agencies. See http://www.uscis.gov/archive/archive-news/fact-sheet-task-force-new-americans. In June 2010 the White House Domestic Policy Council formed the Interagency Working Group on the Federal Role of Immigrant Integration to assess the roles and

equities of the federal government in promoting immigrant integration and to better coordinate integration efforts across agencies. President Barack Obama's proposed 2010 budget included a $10 million allocation for a new Immigrant Integration Program in USCIS' Office of Citizenship that would have established a program devoted exclusively to helping legal immigrants transition into their new communities. See U.S. Government Accountability Office, *Immigrant Integration: U.S. Citizenship and Immigration Services Could Better Assess Its Grant Program*, GAO-12-274, Washington, DC, December 2011.

[112] The White House, Presidential Memorandum, *Creating Welcoming Communities and Fully Integrating Immigrants and Refugees*, November 21, 2014.

[113] S. 744 would have renamed USCIS's Office of Citizenship as the Office of Citizenship and New Americans (OCNA). OCNA's functions would have included promoting institutions and providing training and educational materials on aliens' citizenship responsibilities and providing general leadership, consultation, and coordination of such activities across federal agencies and with state and local entities. In coordination with the Task Force on New Americans (TFNA) established in 2006, OCNA would have: advised USCIS, DHS, and the Domestic Policy Council on challenges related to immigrant integration; established national integration goals; evaluated federal immigrant integration efforts; and identified and assessed integration implications of new and proposed immigration policies. In addition, OCNA would have coordinated with state and local governments on integration issues; coordinated with other federal agencies to do the same regarding education and English programs; assisted states with new immigrant integration grant programs; and required a report to Congress every two years. S. 744 §§2511, 2521-2524.

[114] The White House, Presidential Memorandum, *Creating Welcoming Communities and Fully Integrating Immigrants and Refugees*, November 21, 2014.

[115] See CRS Report R43366, *U.S. Naturalization Policy*, by William A. Kandel.

[116] The INA waives some of these requirements for applicants over age 50 with 20 years of U.S. residency, those with mental or physical disabilities, and those who have served in the U.S. military.

[117] See National Immigration Forum, Making the Naturalization Process Less Daunting by Reforming the USCIS Fee Structure, Washington, DC, 2011; commentary by the United States Conference of Catholic Bishops, Hebrew Immigrant Aid society, and Immigration Policy Center in National Foundation for American Policy, Reforming the Naturalization Process, NFAP Policy Brief, August 2011; and Joyce Baldwin, Helping Immigrants Become U.S. Citizens, Carnegie Corporation of New York, The New Americans Campaign, vol. 7, no. 2, Summer 2013 (hereafter "*Helping Immigrants*, 2013").

[118] Manuel Pastor, Jared Sanchez, and Rhonda Ortiz, et al., Nurturing Naturalization: Could Lowering the Fee Help?, Center for the Study of Immigrant Integration, University of Southern California, February 2013.

[119] See CRS Report R43366, *U.S. Naturalization Policy*, by William A. Kandel, pp. 15-18.

[120] See *Helping Immigrants* 2013 and commentary of the Catholic Conference of Bishops etc. NFAP Policy Brief 2011. Many also characterize the naturalization application forms and instructions as excessively complex and unclear, with potential legal consequences for incorrect responses. They contend that prospective naturalization petitioners may be deterred from applying, and that simplifying the language in the N-400 application and instructions would make the naturalization process more accessible. See commentary of Mary Giovagnoli, Immigration Policy Center, in National Foundation for American Policy, *Reforming the Naturalization Process*, NFAP Policy Brief, August 2011. Others raise concerns over the naturalization residency requirements which disadvantages LPRs based overseas for employment. Such individuals must wait until they physically reside in the United States to fulfill the naturalization requirements, prolonging their time required to naturalize. See commentary of Cyrus D. Mehta and Gary Endelman in National Foundation for American Policy, *Reforming the Naturalization Process*, NFAP Policy Brief, August 2011.

[121] U.S. Department of Homeland Security, Memorandum to Leon Rodriquez, Director, U.S. Citizenship and Immigration Services, from Jeh Charles Johnson, Secretary of Homeland Security, "*Policies to Promote and Increase Access to U.S. Citizenship*," November 20, 2014.

[122] U.S. Citizenship and Immigration Services is almost entirely funded through processing fees, a budgeting approach that contains inherent limitations on how much revenue can be raised to support USCIS operations. See CRS Report RL34040, *U.S. Citizenship and Immigration Services' Immigration Fees and Adjudication Costs: Proposed Adjustments and Historical Context*, by William A. Kandel.

[123] See for example *U.S. Immigration Policy*, 2009, pp. 90-95.

[124] Most recently, for example, S. 744, the Border Security, Economic Opportunity, and Immigration Modernization Act passed by the Senate in 2013, did not include explicit provisions to modernize the administrative functioning and infrastructure of USCIS.

[125] U.S. Department of Homeland Security, Office of Inspector General, *Major Management and Performance Challenges Facing the Department of Homeland Security*, OIG-15-09, November 14, 2014.

[126] The White House, Presidential Memorandum, "Modernizing and Streamlining the U.S. Immigrant Visa System for the 21st Century," November 21, 2014.

[127] Jeffrey S. Passel and D'Vera Cohn, *Unauthorized Immigrant Totals Rise in 7 States, Fall in 14: Decline in Those From Mexico Fuels Most State Decreases*, Pew Research Center, Washington, DC, November 18, 2014, p. 8. In 2012, the size of the civilian labor force was estimated at 157.7 million according to data from the 2012 American Community Survey. See "Factfinder" at Census.gov.

[128] For example, see Southern Policy Law Center, "Immigrant Justice," http://www.splcenter.org/what-we-do/immigrant-justice.

[129] Ibid.

[130] Unauthorized workers represents relatively large proportions of the workforce in particular industries, such as agriculture, construction, food handling, and low-skilled services. Jeffrey S Passel and D'Vera Cohn, *A Portrait of Unauthorized Immigrants in the United States*, Pew Research Center, Washington, DC, April 14, 2009.

[131] INA §274A. These cases also may involve additional violations, such as alien smuggling, document fraud, and worker exploitation. See. CRS Report R40002, *Immigration-Related Worksite Enforcement: Performance Measures*, by Andorra Bruno.

[132] U.S. Department of Homeland Security, USCIS fact sheet, *Worksite Enforcement Overview*, April 30, 2009.

[133] U.S. Department of Labor, *Revised Memorandum of Understanding between the Departments of Homeland Security and Labor Concerning Enforcement Activities at Worksites*, December 11, 2011.

[134] See for instance, National Immigration Law Center, "DHS Issues "New" Worksite Enforcement Guidelines That Are Simply More of the Same," press release, April 30, 2009.

[135] Thomas E. Perez, Secretary, U.S. Department of Labor, "Fact Sheet: Establishment of Interagency Working Group for the Consistent Enforcement of Federal Labor, Employment and Immigration Laws," November 21, 2014.

[136] For more on U and T statuses, see CRS Report RL34317, *Trafficking in Persons: U.S. Policy and Issues for Congress*, by Alison Siskin and Liana Rosen.

[137] Department of Homeland Security U.S. Citizenship and Immigration Services, Information for Law Enforcement Officials, *Immigration Relief for Victims of Human Trafficking and Other Crimes*, http://www.uscis.gov/sites/default/files/USCIS/ Resources/Humanitarian%20Based%20Benefits%20and%20Resources/TU_QAforLawEnforcement.pdf.

[138] Current policy allows DOL's Wage and Hour Division to certify trafficking victims for U status. While trafficking victims may be eligible for U status, only victims of severe forms of trafficking may qualify for T status. Department of Labor, *The Department of Labor's Wage and Hour Division Will Expand Its Support Of Victims of Human Trafficking and*

Other Crimes Seeking Immigration Relief from DHS, Fact Sheet, Washington, DC, November 20, 2014 ; and Department of Labor, "Secretary's Order 01-2014," vol. 79, no. 247 *Federal Register* 30224, December 24, 2014.

[139] Since 2011, DOL has provided law enforcement certification for U visa applications for the following crimes: trafficking, involuntary servitude, peonage, obstruction of justice, and witness tampering.

[140] For example, see Alliance to End Slavery and Trafficking, *DOL/Department of Wage and Hour, The Need for Funding and Report Language: $5,000,000 for services for victims of trafficking to implement Section 107(b) of the TVPA and report language*, http://endslaveryandtrafficking.org/fy2014/Department-of-Labor-Department-of-Wage-and-Hour.php.

In: Immigration Policy Proposals ...
Editor: Kimberly D. Parsons

ISBN: 978-1-63482-344-9

Chapter 4

H.R. 5759, PREVENTING EXECUTIVE OVERREACH ON IMMIGRATION ACT OF 2014*

Douglas W. Elmendorf

Honorable Pete Sessions
Chairman
Committee on Rules
U.S. House of Representatives
Washington, DC 20515

Dear Mr. Chairman:

As requested, CBO and the staff of the Joint Committee on Taxation (JCT) have analyzed H.R. 5759, the Preventing Executive Overreach on Immigration Act of 2014, as amended and posted on the website of the House Committee on Rules on December 2, 2014. The legislation would prohibit the executive branch from exempting or deferring from removal certain categories of aliens considered to be unlawfully present in the United States. It also would prohibit the executive branch from treating those people as if they were

* This is an edited, reformatted and augmented version of a document issued by the Congressional Budget Office, December 2014.

lawfully present or had lawful immigration status, or providing those people with the authorization to work legally.

CBO and JCT expect that enacting the proposed amendment in the nature of a substitute for H.R. 5759 would reduce both revenues and outlays for direct spending programs. However, because of the short time available since the President announced his action, CBO and JCT cannot provide a specific estimate of those effects at this time. Moreover, because the effects on revenues and outlays would be at least partially offsetting, CBO and JCT cannot currently determine whether the legislation would increase or decrease federal budget deficits over the next 10 years. (The legislation could also have effects on spending subject to appropriation, but CBO cannot determine the extent or direction of those effects on discretionary spending.)

EFFECTS ON DIRECT SPENDING

Under the bill, participation in several programs would decline because some people would no longer be eligible to participate or because they would choose not to participate for fear of revealing their unlawful presence. CBO and JCT expect that spending for the following programs would be reduced if the legislation was enacted:

Earned Income Tax Credit (EITC). To receive an EITC, an individual must have a valid Social Security number (SSN). Those people affected by the bill would not be able to apply for an SSN and thus would not be eligible to receive the EITC.

- *Additional Child Tax Credit (ACTC).* To receive an ACTC, or refundable child tax credit, a taxpayer must have a certain amount of earned income. As some individuals would reduce their reported employment income, they may qualify for fewer refundable child tax credits.
- *Social Security and Medicare.* To collect Social Security and Medicare benefits while in the United States, an individual must be lawfully present. Under the bill those people who would no longer be lawfully present would be ineligible to receive such benefits. Over the 2015-2024 period, relatively few of the people affected by the bill would have reached the eligibility ages for Social Security old-age benefits or for Medicare. Some of the affected people would have

become eligible for Social Security disability benefits and for Medicare based on their disability status.

- *Other Federal Benefits.* Many of the people who would be affected by the legislation have children who are natural-born U.S. citizens. Those children, like other citizens, are eligible for federal benefits if they meet the relevant eligibility criteria for particular programs. CBO expects that some of those children's parents who would apply for benefits on their children's behalf under the President's deferral actions would opt not to apply for such benefits if H.R. 5759 was enacted because they would fear revealing their own unlawful presence.

EFFECTS ON REVENUES

The proposed amendment in the nature of a substitute for H.R. 5759 would affect tax revenues in a number of ways, some of which would decrease receipts and some of which would increase them. After accounting for all of the effects, JCT expects that enacting the legislation would reduce tax revenues.

JCT expects that the legislation would result in reduced reporting of employment income by people who, under the President's executive order, will be treated as lawfully present or authorized to work. That decrease in reported wages would cause decreases in receipts from both individual income taxes and payroll taxes.

If you wish further details about this letter, we will be pleased to provide them. The CBO staff contact is Melissa Merrell.

Sincerely,
Douglas W. Elmendorf
Director

cc: Honorable Louise M. Slaughter
Ranking Member

Honorable Ted S. Yoho

INDEX

C

D

E

F

G

H

I

J

L

M

N

O

P

Q

R

S

V

W